How to Write Critical Essays
A guide for students of literature

How to write critical essays

A guide for students of literature

David B. Pirie

London and New York

First published in 1985 by
Methuen & Co. Ltd
Reprinted 1986 (twice)

Reprinted 1989, 1990, 1991 by
Routledge
11 New Fetter Lane, London EC4P 4EE
29 West 35th Street, New York, NY 1001

Photoset by Rowland Phototypesetting Ltd
Bury St Edmunds, Suffolk
Printed in England by Clays Ltd, St Ives plc

British Library Cataloguing in Publication Data

Pirie, David B.
    How to write critical essays:
    a guide for students of literature.
    1. Criticism
    I. Title
    801'.95   PN81
    ISBN 0-415-04533-9

Library of Congress Cataloging in Publication Data

Pirie, David.
  · How to write critical essays.
    1. Criticism   I. Title.
    PN81.P54 1985   808'.0668   84-27259
    ISBN 0-415-04533-9 (pbk.)

Contents

Introduction

There are so many practical suggestions in this book that you are almost certain to find some of them useful if you want your essays to gain higher marks. But I am assuming that you want more than that. If you have no worthier aim than impressing your teachers, essay-writing will at best seem a bore. At worst it will induce panic.

The process of researching, planning and writing a critical essay can, and should, be enjoyable. If, at present, the prospect of such an exercise seems either dismal or daunting, that is almost certainly because you have not yet thought hard enough about your own aims in writing criticism. So this book will pose some of the questions which you need to ponder if you are ever to discover what is, for you, the purpose and pleasure in composing critical essays.

Such questions inevitably depend on larger ones about the value of literature itself. These in turn raise even trickier issues about language, the human mind and the social structures within which we live and think. Some sections of this guide outline some of the theoretical questions that you need to consider. In such limited space, I have been able to give only the briefest account of each, even of those questions to which entire books have been devoted. You may therefore find certain passages frustratingly simplistic or irritatingly partisan. Provided that you are then provoked into thinking out your own more subtle or balanced formulation, you will still benefit.

But if many of the ideas here are wholly new to you, you may find the brevity merely baffling. Persevere for a while. Many university teachers, including myself, find some of these issues uncomfortably challenging and you should feel no shame in having to progress carefully on such difficult terrain. Nevertheless, if you repeatedly get lost in one of the more theoretical sections, give it up for the time being and go on to read the rest of the book. You will find that even in sections discussing the most practical aspects of the essay-writing process, issues of broad principle are often raised, if only implicitly.

Whenever a critical technique – even one which, to the hasty glance of common sense, seems merely functional – is being deployed or recommended, major assumptions about the nature of literature and the purpose of criticism are being made. Any critical practice implies a principle. Since the most practical sections are designed to be clear and concise, I have sometimes had to give advice about methodology without spelling out the ways in which a particular method will make your essay tacitly support one set of assumptions rather than another. At many points, however, it has proved possible to indicate briefly some of the alternative theories which under-pin different essay-writing styles. You may find that these passages, grounded as they are in specific examples of choices that the essay-writer must make, clarify those issues which had seemed to you elusively abstract when you first met them in one of the more theoretical passages. If so, you should eventually be able to return to such a passage and make more sense of it.

However diligently you read, or even reread, this book, it cannot provide you with a guaranteed recipe for the good essay. Anyone who tells you that religious observance of a few simple rules will ensure success is either a fool or is patron-izingly treating you as one. Of course, there are many recom-mendations in the following pages which seem to me almost indisputably right and likely to have the support of nearly all literature teachers. Nevertheless, at many other points where, to save space and time, I must sound just as baldly prescrip-tive, your own or your teacher's preferences may differ from mine. Thoughtful critics have always disagreed about what criticism should seek to achieve and which methods it should employ. But the variety of approaches now being offered by scholars, critics and theorists, and the vigour with which their debate is being conducted, are quite unprecedented. So at many points, this book will not give you unequivocal guidance. Instead it will help you to make your own definition of what constitutes a good essay.

Your confidence about that, like your skill in deploying your own choice of the various techniques discussed, is bound to be limited at first. It will grow only with practice. You will learn much from the advice of your teachers, the example (good or bad) of published criticism, discussion with your fellow students and, of course, your steadily deepening experience of an ever wider range of literary texts. Yet it will be the actual experience of writing essays which will teach you most about both the possibilities and the pitfalls of composing critical prose.

For such practice there is no substitute and this book does not pretend to be one. The chapters that follow cannot tell you what should be said about a literary topic. They can, however, help you to decide what you want to say and they will show you how to say it clearly in a style and format which your reader will welcome.

1 Facing the question

This chapter will be of most use when you have been given a specific question to answer. But even when you have been asked simply to 'write an essay on', you should find help here. Some passages will prove suggestive, as you try to think of issues that may be worth raising. Others will show you how these can then be further defined and developed.

Decode the question systematically

If you just glance at a set question and then immediately start to wonder how you will answer it, you are unlikely to produce an interesting essay, let alone a strictly relevant one. To write interesting criticism you need to read well. That means, among many other things, noticing words, exploring their precise implications, and weighing their usefulness in a particular context. You may as well get in some early practice by analysing your title. There are anyway crushingly self-evident advantages in being sure that you do understand a demand before you put effort into trying to fulfil it.

Faced by any question of substantial length, you should make the first entry in your notes a restatement, in your own words, of what your essay is required to do. To this you should constantly refer throughout the process of assembling material, planning your answer's structure, and writing the essay. Since the sole aim of this reformulation is to assist your own understanding and memory, you can adopt whatever method seems to you most clarifying. Here is one:

1) Write out at the top of the first page of your notes the full question exactly as set.
2) Circle the words that seem to you essential.
3) Write above each of the words or phrases which you have circled either a capital 'S' for 'Subject' or a capital 'A' for 'Approach'.
4) Place in square brackets any of the still unmarked words which, though not absolutely essential to an understanding of the title's major demands, seem to you potentially helpful in thinking towards your essay.
5) Cross out any word or phrase which, after prudently patient thought, still strikes you as mere grammar or decoration or padding.

Here is an example:

> 'We all of us, grave or light, get our thoughts entangled in metaphors and act fatally on the strength of them' (*Middlemarch*). Discuss the function of metaphor in George Eliot's work.

This might become:

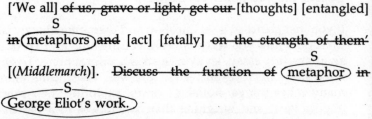

The choices I have made here are, of course, debatable.

For instance, some of the words that I have crossed out may strike you as just useful enough to be allowed to survive within square brackets. Presumably, you agree that 'Discuss' adds nothing to the demands that any essay-writer would anticipate even before looking at the specific terms of a given question; but what about 'grave or light'? Might retention of that phrase help you to focus on George Eliot's tone, its range over different works, or its variability within one? Do metaphors play such a large part in signalling shifts of tone that the alternation of gravity and lightheartedness is a relevant issue?

And what about the phrase 'function of'? Clearly no essay could usefully discuss devices like metaphors without considering the way in which they work, the effect they have upon the reader, and the role that they play relative to other components in a particular text. Nevertheless, you might decide to retain the phrase as a helpful reminder that such issues must apply here as elsewhere.

You may wonder why '(*Middlemarch*)' has not been circled. The quotation does happen to be from what many regard as George Eliot's best novel but in fact there is no suggestion that your essay should centre upon that particular work. The title mentions it, in parentheses, only to supply the source of the quotation and thus save those who do not recognize it from wasting time in baffled curiosity. It does, however, seem worth retaining in square brackets. It will remind you to find the relevant passage of the novel and explore the original context. You can predict that the quoted sentence follows or precedes some example of the kind of metaphor which the novel itself regards as deserving comment. Less importantly, the person destined to read your essay has apparently found that passage memorable.

Deciding how to mark a title will not just discipline you into noticing what it demands. It should reassure you, at least in the case of such relatively long questions, that you can already identify issues which deserve further investigation. It thus prevents that sterile panic in which you doubt your ability to think of anything at all to say in your essay. If you tend to suffer from such doubts, make a few further notes immediately after you have reformulated the question. The essential need is to record some of the crucial issues while you have them in mind. Your immediate jottings to counter future writer's block might in this case include some of the following points, though you could, of course, quite legitimately make wholly different ones.

KEY-TERM QUERIES

'metaphors'/metaphor:
Quote suggests we 'all' think in metaphors but title concentrates demand on metaphor as literary device in G.E.'s written 'work': how relate/discriminate these two?

How easy in G.E. to distinguish metaphor from mere simile on one hand and overall symbolism on other?

G.E.'s work:
No guidance on how few or many texts required but 'work' broad enough to suggest need of range. Any major differences between ways metaphors are used in, say, *Middlemarch, Mill on the Floss & Silas Marner?*
'work' does not confine essay to novels: use some short stories (*Scenes from Clerical Life?*)? Check what G.E. wrote in other genres.
How characterize *G.E.*'s use of metaphor? Distinguish from other (contemporary?) novelists?

HELPFUL HINT QUERIES

Middlemarch (quote):
More/less systematically structured on metaphors than other G.E. novels?
Find localized context of quote. What is last metaphor used by text before this generalization and what first after? Do these clarify/alter implications of quote?

'We all':
G.E. *does* keep interrupting story to offer own general observations. Metaphors part of same generalizing process? Or do metaphors bridge gap between concretes of story & abstracts of authorial comment?
How many of text's crucial metaphors evoke recurring patterns in which *all* human minds shape their thoughts? How many define more distinctive mental habits of particular characters?

'thoughts':
G.E. sometimes called an unusually intellectual novelist. What of text's own 'thoughts' in relation to those supposedly in minds of individual characters? Where/how distinguishable?
Text's more generalized 'thoughts' may not just illuminate plot & characters. They may be part of self-portrait by which it constructs itself as a personalized voice. Do they persuade us we're meeting an inspiringly shrewd person rather than just reading an entertaining book?

'entangled':
Word is itself metaphorical. Various connotations: inter-woven/confused/constricted?
What is entangled in what? Characters in their metaphor-defined ideas of each other, or of society, or of own past?
Many spider's web metaphors in *Middlemarch*. Are these different from river images in *Mill on the Floss* or is being 'entangled' much the same as being 'carried along by current'?

'act':
Plot? Are main narrative events described by frequent or powerful use of metaphor?
Where does G.E. offer more specific demonstrations that characters do think in metaphors and act accordingly?
Could 'act' be a pun? We act upon metaphors in our heads as helplessly as actors conform to lines of scripts? (incidentally, are some G.E. scenes theatrical & is the staginess of some dialogues caused by characters having to pronounce sus-piciously well-turned metaphors?)

'fatally':
Usefully equivocal?
(a) Some G.E. metaphors do suggest a character's behaviour is predetermined: we're all fated to act within limits imposed by our upbringing, our earlier actions & pressures of society.
(b) Other G.E. metaphors expand to tragic resolutions of whole plots which prove *literally* fatal for major characters. Metaphorical river flowing through *Mill on Floss* grows to drowning flood (literal & symbolic) of last pages in which hero & heroine die. (Incidentally, is Tom the only hero? What of Stephen? Do metaphors help to signal who matters most?)

These notes may look dauntingly numerous and full, consider-ing that they are meant to represent first thoughts on review-ing the title. Of course, I have not been able to use as economi-cally abbreviated notes as you could safely write when only you need to understand them. Nevertheless, you could obviously not write as much as this unless you already knew some of the texts. Even if you are in that fortunate position when first given a title, you may not want, or feel able, to write so much at this very first stage of the essay-preparation pro-cess. Nevertheless, you should always be able to find some issues worth raising at the outset so that, when you embark on your research, you have already jotted down some points that may be worth pursuing.

Notice how often the above examples use question marks. You may later decide – as you read and think more – that some of the problems that first occurred to you should not be discussed in your essay. Even those confirmed as relevant by growing knowledge of the texts will need to be defined far more precisely and fully before you think about composing paragraphs.

Notice too that in a number of cases the issues have emerged through wondering whether any of the question's terms might have more than one meaning. Investigation of ambiguity can often stir the blank mind into discovering relevant questions.

Terms of approach

You may spot easily enough the keywords in which a title defines your subject-matter but terms prescribing how this is to be approached may prove harder to find. Often they are simply not there. Essay-writing should, after all, exercise your own skills in designing some appropriate style and form in which to define and explore a given literary problem.

Even where a title's grammar is imperative rather than interrogative, you will usually have to decide for yourself how the topic should be tackled. The title may tell you to 'Describe', 'Discuss', 'Debate', 'Analyse', 'Interpret', 'Compare' or 'Evaluate'. In all these cases, you are still being asked questions: what do you think are the most relevant issues here? what is the most appropriate evidence which needs to be weighed in investigating them? how should that evidence be presented and on what premises should it be evaluated?

When your essay title uses one of the above imperatives, you must not assume that the demands represented by the others can be ignored. Many students are, for instance, misled by titles which tell them merely to 'Describe' some feature of a text. They think this sounds a less intellectually strenuous assignment than one which requires them to 'Discuss' or 'Debate'. They may offer a mere recital of facts rather than an argument about their significance. But the text which you are to describe will often be one which your reader already knows intimately. How you approach and assess even its most obvious features may be of interest to your tutor. The mere fact that these features exist will not. Description in a critical essay must initiate and contribute to debate. To 'Describe' is in fact to 'Discuss'. To discuss intelligently is to be specific, to observe details, to identify the various parts which together determine a work's overall impact. So you must 'Analyse' even where the title's imperatives do not explicitly include that demand.

Conversely, your being told merely to 'Interpret' a play or a novel would still require you to analyse the episodes into which it structures its story, the patterns by which it groups its personages, the distinct idioms through which it identifies their speech patterns and the recurring terms and images which compel all the characters to share its recognizably unified discourse. Interpretation must, of course, expose the ethical, religious or political value systems which a text implicitly reinforces or subverts. Yet these exist• only in the architecture of its form and in the building materials of its language. What Shakespeare's *Julius Caesar*, for instance, is encouraging us to believe cannot be shown by a superficial summary of its plot. Such a summary might be almost identical with that of the original prose version of the story which Shakespeare found in North's translation of Plutarch.

Where Shakespeare's *Julius Caesar* does subtly deviate from its source, it suppresses some of the basic narrative's latent implications and foregrounds others. So interpretation of just how a particular work seeks to manipulate our definitions of what is true or desirable may also require you to make comparisons. You can hardly have sufficient sense of direction to know where one text is pushing you if your map of literature has no landmarks, and includes no texts which outline some alternative path. Thus, even where an essay title does not explicitly require you to approach one set text by reference to another, you are almost certain to find comparisons useful.

'Compare' – even where it is not immediately followed by 'and contrast' – does not mean that you should simply find the common ground between two texts. You must look for dissimilarities as well as similarities. The more shrewdly discriminating your reading of both texts has been, the more your comparison will reveal points at which there is a difference of degree, if not of kind.

Nevertheless, you must wonder what the relatively few works which are regarded as literature do have in common. Your essay is bound to imply some theory as to why these should be studied and what distinguishes them from the vast majority of printed texts.

Student essays sometimes suggest that literature is composed of fictional and imaginative texts, and excludes those which aim to be directly factual or polemical. An English Literature syllabus, however, may include Shakespeare's plays about political history and Donne's sermons while excluding those often highly imaginative works which most of your fellow citizens prefer to read: science fiction, for instance, or pornography or historical romances or spy stories.

Alternatively, the focus of your essay may imply that the works which can be discussed profitably in critical prose share an alertness to language; that we can recognize a literary work because it appears at least as interested in the style through which it speaks as in the meaning which it conveys. Yet many of the texts which criticism scornfully ignores – the lyrics of popular songs, advertising slogans, journalistic essays – often play games with words and draw as much attention to signifier as to signified. There is now vigorous controversy as to which of the many available rationales – if any – does stand up to rational examination. Recognize the view which each critical method implicitly supports, and choose accordingly.

'Evaluate' may also be already implicit in each of the other imperatives which tend to recur in essay titles. Description without any sense of priorities would be shapeless and never-ending. Discussion must be based on some sense of what matters. Analysis may involve a search for the significant among the relatively trivial. Interpretation of a text, and even more obviously comparison of it with another, tends to work – however tentatively – towards some judgement as to the relative importance of what it has to say and the degree of skill with which it says it.

Conversely, evaluative judgements only become criticism when they are grounded upon accurate description of the work which is being praised or condemned. If such judgements are to be sufficiently precise to be clear and sufficiently well supported to be convincing, they must be seen to derive from observant analysis of the work's components. They must also show sufficient knowledge of other texts to demonstrate by comparison exactly what about this one seems to you relatively impressive or unimpressive. So, too, they must be based on an energetic curiosity about the overall ideological pressure which a text exerts as the cumulative result of its more localized effects. You cannot decide whether to admire a text as an illuminating resource or to condemn it as a mystifying obstruction until you have worked out what ways of thinking it is trying to expand or contain. To evaluate, you must interpret.

These interrelated concepts of evaluation and interpretation are, as the next section explains, more intriguingly problematical than some critics acknowledge.

Some problems of value and meaning

Can the values of a literary work be equally accessible to all its readers? Is a given meaning which interpretative criticism extracts likely to seem as meaningful to one reader as to another, and to remain unaffected by any difference in their respective situations? To take an admittedly extreme example, could a book about slavery – whether it supported or opposed that system – make such equally convincing sense to both slaves and slave-owners that they would be able to agree on just how good a text it was?

At least in those days when there was still major controversy over whether the slave trade should be eliminated, criticism ought presumably to have anticipated quite different responses to the same text. You might protest, however, that even then there were few slave-owners, and still fewer slaves, among those authors who contributed to the debate; or among the contemporary reviewers who evaluated their works; or among the readers for whom both authors and reviewers wrote. Literature at that time, you might argue, was in fact produced, processed and consumed by a class which had little direct experience of the business world that made its leisure possible. If that were your contention, you might usefully wonder about the relevance of literary values if they can be created, at least in some periods, by those far removed from society's key-situations.

The notion of an isolated and relatively ignorant circle of writers and readers would anyway need investigating. Jane Austen was well enough informed about the origins of wealth in her own circle to write *Mansfield Park*, in which Sir Thomas Bertram has to be absent from his English estate so that he can check up on his apparently more essential investments in the sugar plantations of the West Indies. This does not, of course, prevent his being respected by some modern interpretations as the text's moral touchstone. By contrast, another author of the period, Thomas Love Peacock, used more than one of his novels to attack the West Indies trade explicitly. His own commitment had led him to join those who refused to eat sugar on the grounds that its popularity made slaving profitable. One of his novels devotes some of its liveliest prose to arguing that the reader should do likewise.

How far a contemporary reader interpreted the relevant passages in both novelists' works as offering central, rather than merely peripheral, meanings might depend in part on the amount of space actually given to them. However, you know from your own experience as a critical reader of novels that merely counting the number of paragraphs or pages devoted to a particular issue settles few questions about a text's deeper pattern of emphases and fluctuating intensities. So perhaps the judgement of some readers at the time was influenced by whether they themselves had investments in the West Indies; or at least by how much the social circles in which they moved had a taste for sugar and could afford to satisfy it.

You may concede that in the eighteenth century a peasant and an aristocrat would have been right to decide that admiration for a particular text would be unlikely to serve both their interests. Nevertheless you may see this as a problem that the modern critic is spared. You may believe that the gap between rich and poor has now become so negligibly slight that we can all afford to share a common code of values whose acceptance is of no more advantage to one group than another. You may feel that, as free citizens of an egalitarian society, we can now all benefit equally from a text's being interpreted in a given way, or evaluated so highly that it exerts a powerful influence. If your essay does imply this, it may be adopting an essentially political stance. Your prose may be quietly insisting that the present forms of society are so admirably fair that they should be conserved rather than challenged.

Your essay may anyway imply that texts which argue a point of view about slavery – or indeed any other economic system – are not likely to be among the great works of art on which criticism should concentrate. In judging a work of literature, or in trying to identify its central meaning, we should focus, according to some critics, on far more important topics than social injustice: ultimately politics do not matter; personal feelings – which are supposedly unaffected by political structures – do. But this idea may itself be highly political. If people of vastly different wealth and power were still liable to suffer much the same pain and could still manage to enjoy much the same pleasure, would there be any great point in struggling for social reform? Where the same essential, enduring human experiences are already equally available to all, why change the circumstances in which some of us still have to live?

Let us suppose, for instance, that early productions of *Hamlet* affected all members of the audience in much the same way; that even the most socially disadvantaged felt as sympathetic to the hero as did the most privileged. Both groups might then have seen class warfare as utterly irrelevant. Pauper and prince might feel that their real enemies were not each other but those supposedly universal problems which pose an equal threat to everyone's happiness and sanity: loneliness, for instance, or fear of death, or a despairing sense that love never lasts and existence has no ultimate point or purpose.

If the play was originally valued for such meanings, it may have played its own small part in preventing progress. It may have helped to delay that recognition of conflicting interests which eventually led ordinary men and women to demand the vote, and so gain some chance of influencing the ways in which they were governed.

Let us assume that you believe in democracy and accept at least the possibility that *Hamlet* has had that kind of negative influence in the past. How far should such considerations determine your own present choices as to what meanings in the play your interpretation should foreground and what qualities your evaluation should praise?

Titles may imply premises which you should question

Think before you accept any assumptions which a title implicitly makes. It is your job to weigh their soundness before deciding whether an answer can be safely based upon them. Here is an easy example: '"*Richard II*, being such an intimately personal tragedy, is poignantly moving; yet it has moments which do succeed in being genuinely funny." Discuss.' You must ask yourself whether the text succeeds in being poignant, and you must also answer the question of whether it is funny. 'Personal', too, should ring loud alarm bells. Is this really a potentially sentimental story about one idiosyncratic person or is it a latently polemical tale about an entire society? Presumably political events can be tragic in their effect on groups as well as on individuals.

The less obviously contentious word here is 'tragedy'. Yet many readers of *Richard II* have thought 'history play' an apter description of it. When writing on this subject, you would have to decide which category you think the play belongs to. Indeed you might have to explore many of the issues raised by another examination question on the play: 'In what precise sense could the term "tragedy" be applied to *Richard II* and how far is it an adequate description?'

'Tragedy' is sometimes used neutrally to identify a genre (though even then definitions vary enormously) but it is sometimes offered evaluatively to imply a relative superiority. You might be asked to discuss the idea that 'Marlowe's *Tamburlaine* is an adventure story rather than a tragedy'. This may strike you as merely descriptive unless you are too snooty to admire the literature of action and suspense. When, however, you are told that '*Macbeth* is not so much a tragedy as a gory melodrama', you may suspect that the title is condemning artistic failure rather than identifying the class of literature to which the play belongs. Perhaps you should rescue even 'melodrama' and 'melodramatic' from their derogatory connotations. To assume that whole genres of literature are by definition more or less significant is dangerous. It may make you accept too uncritically the importance of some texts and dismiss others too quickly as trivial.

The premises of the literary establishment tend to suggest, for instance, that 'epic' is always to be applauded: essay titles inviting you to decide whether a work is an epic may imply that the issue is almost synonymous with whether it is great: '"Far from fulfilling its pretensions to epic, Hardy's *The Dynasts* is clumsily constructed and colourlessly executed." Discuss.' Here you should, of course, discuss the implicit claim that there cannot be an incompetent epic, whereas a sonnet, for example, however atrociously written, remains a sonnet.

Journalism, on the other hand, tends to have a bad press in essay titles (with a few perhaps arbitrary exceptions for writers such as Samuel Johnson or Walter Pater). Consider the evaluative premises lurking here: '"Defoe does not deserve to be called the first English novelist. His fictions are thinly-veiled essays in social analysis by an author who was little more than an investigative reporter." Do you agree?' You must not only decide how far you accept that Defoe's major works belong in one genre rather than another. You also need to work out whether the texts prove that journalistic analysis of society is innately more trivial than novel-writing. You might even wish to define the genre of the novel as narrative fiction which is indeed centred on 'social analysis' and not on 'personal relationships' or whatever you suspect the title of suggesting.

So you may find it useful in reformulating titles to put a capital 'T' for tendentious above any term which seems to you to be more manipulative than it might at first appear. You can also place a capital 'P' above any word or phrase which you think discreetly infiltrates a premise which your essay must question.

Short titles may require long and complex answers

Systematic discrimination between a title's crucial terms and its irrelevantly decorative verbiage should allow you to spot the lengthy questions which are merely long-winded and the succinct ones which actually make as great, or greater, demands. Consider, for example, 'Was Pope a true wit or merely an imitator of others?' 'Wit' is a notoriously unstable term, shifting its emphases throughout the history of the language. In the past the concept had far more to do with cleverness and less with comedy. Obviously, 'true' is the least qualifying of epithets since it begs all the questions about what the writer takes truth to be.

Circling of key-terms would, however, stress 'imitator' and reveal that the title includes originality as one of the essential ingredients of 'wit'. Thus a title which at first might seem to have Pope as its subject in fact insists upon your comparing his work with that of his predecessors and contemporaries.

This inclusion of novelty within the definition of 'wit' does not, however, exclude its other connotations. Your answer would also have to consider at least Pope's verbal dexterity and precision, his intellectual subtlety and his sense of humour.

Conversely, a title may sound more demanding than it actually is. Its syntax may divide into two apparently distinct questions which, once the key-terms have been identified and explored, resolve themselves into only one: 'How do you account for the view, frequently expressed, that *King Lear* is "a poor stage play"? What steps would you take to defend the play from the imputation that it is unlikely to do well in the theatre?' The first sentence's 'poor stage play' and the second's 'unlikely to do well in the theatre' pose the same possibility and specify only one subject for your essay to explore. The terms of approach here seem merely to restate a long-established rule: whenever you give an account of the grounds on which a text may be attacked, you ought also to consider those steps that other commentators might take in mounting a defence.

Most students in reformulating the question would probably cross out many of the opening words: 'How do you account for the view, frequently expressed'. They would assume that the whole title can be translated as '*King Lear* is a poor stage play. Discuss.' Their answers would be confined to the supposedly innate weaknesses and strengths of the text itself. Nevertheless, some students might see in the opening words an invitation to consider the motives, conscious or unconscious, which have led some critics to construct the text in particular ways.

Was Bradley (*Shakespearean Tragedy*, London, 1904), for instance, committed to depoliticizing literature when he argued that the battle-scenes make for clumsy theatre? Was he implying that civil war and the question of who rules England are innately less worthy as topics for great drama than personal relationships? Then there are those Christian critics who have protested at the difficulty of staging Gloucester's blinding. Could this be because they fear that the impact of eyeballs being torn out might make an audience reject the belief that physical suffering can do good so long as it leads to spiritual regeneration? But you may believe that a text contains for all time some unaltering value or meaning. Then you are bound to see the ideological pressures on criticism as hardly worth discussion. You will assume that the best critics are motivated only by a desire to see what has always been actually present in the text itself; the worst may be trying to press it into serving some non-literary cause, but they presumably do not deserve consideration.

If, by contrast, you believe that the qualities and import of a text are constantly being redefined and that all criticism is bound to be creative production, then you will feel that to 'account for' those views of a text which have been 'frequently expressed' during some period of a text's history is often crucial. You may even think that a major justification of literary study is that the history of critical interpretations can reveal how those with cultural influence have dominated in the past, and so alert you to some of the contemporary pressures under which you do the thinking and writing which are supposedly your own. Whether you think that your essay should discuss such topics must partly depend, of course, on how you interpret the terms of the set question since relevance to its demands is a major priority. But it is not the only one. Here, as so often, your decision as to whether certain issues should be tackled will also depend on your own theories about literature and criticism.

Titles may tell you how much you need to read

'Write an essay on *King Lear*' clearly means that your priority is to answer the question: how attentively have you read *King Lear*? Yet it may also pose the following questions about your reading: have you found any other works illuminating in assessing that play? did any other plays by Shakespeare or his contemporaries prove helpful as comparisons? did any literary work of some other period or genre seem relevant? what critical books or essays stimulated your own thoughts?

Another example of a title which seems to choose your reading for you might be: 'Evaluate Leavis's criticism of Shelley's "Ode to the West Wind".' Obviously you must study that poem and the passage in chapter six of F. R. Leavis's *Revaluations* (London, 1936) which attacks it. But your tutor may also be asking: what other critical responses to the Ode have you read? which of these seemed to you more or less persuasive than Leavis's and why? which other essays by Leavis himself have you read, and did they help you to identify any recurrent premises or prejudices which can be seen at work in his rejection of Shelley? which other poems of Shelley have you read and did they suggest to you that Leavis's chosen example was fair or misleadingly untypical?

Your tutor may give you a range of essay titles from which to choose. Then you must calculate how much preparatory reading each would require before you make your selection.

If, for instance, you have previously read only one of Dickens's novels and have limited time, it is obvious which of the following questions you should attempt:

(a) Write a detailed analysis of one chapter from any of Dickens's novels and show how far its subject-matter and style typify the rest of the book.

(b) 'Dickens's earlier works are competent but lack originality. It is only in the later novels that we can hear that distinctively subtle voice which makes most other Victorian novelists sound ponderous.' Discuss.

Adequate reading for (b) would include at least two 'earlier works' and at least two 'later novels' since the plural is used in both phrases. Yet it is the demand for knowledge of a majority of other Victorian novelists which would defeat most students. You would need to have read at least one novel by nearly every major novelist of the period before you could form a judgement on whether their works sound relatively ponderous.

So too an essay on 'Tennyson's originality' should only be attempted by someone who knows – or has time to get to know – the Romantic verse which had been published in the decades before Tennyson's first volume, *Poems by Two Brothers* (1830).

At the opposite extreme you might be asked to 'write a

critical appreciation' of just one short poem. Even here, however, you must think out how much reading will be necessary. Some poems cannot be sensibly treated in isolation from others. There are, for instance, poems which were written and published as matching pairs. Browning's enthusiastically erotic 'Meeting at Night' belongs with his cynically sexist 'Parting at Morning' in a carefully wrought confrontation. Even more obviously, a parody can only be evaluated by reference to its target. The notes in a good edition, or sufficiently detailed works of criticism, should alert you to what else you may need to read. It might also be prudent to ask your tutor for an opinion as to which analogous poems, if any, are essential.

Even when you have made sure that the named poem does not demand knowledge of others, check that the terms of the question do allow you to concentrate exclusively on the specified work. If, for instance, you are asked to show how 'typical' it is of verse written in its time or how 'characteristic' it is of its author, you must clearly demonstrate that you have read enough other poems.

These demands may not always be obvious. Consider the following questions, all of which require you to discuss more poems than the one specified:

> Analyse 'The Wreck of the Deutschland' to show whether Hopkins is most illuminatingly read as a Victorian or as a modern poet.

> 'The Rape of the Lock''s unflagging energy, its consistently witty style and unshakeably lucid structure, ensure that it is Pope's one truly lasting achievement.' Discuss.

> 'The balance of tradition against experiment.' How appropriate do you think this is as a description of any one poem of the period?

The first of these requires knowledge of poems by other writers who, like Hopkins, lived in the Victorian period. An answer to the second would need to consider other poems by Pope before it could decide whether 'The Rape of the Lock' so certainly surpassed them. In the third question, 'tradition' presumably means the literary convention established by many other poems.

No points, of course, can be scored for having read works which are unrelated to the set topic. You may indeed lose marks because irrelevant knowledge wastes time and muffles clarity. Nevertheless, tutors are bound to favour a student who is sufficiently enthusiastic and interested to have read widely. So where you cannot decide whether a text is sufficiently relevant, come down on the side of discussing it. On balance it is better to be suspected of gratuitous showing off than of laziness.

The one suspicion which you must never arouse is, of course, that of lying. If you have not read a book it is silly to imply that you have. The childish dishonesty which is sometimes inflicted on schoolteachers will be strongly re-sented by any tutor who means to treat you as an adult.

Remember, anyway, that breadth of reading is only one of the many qualities that your essay may need to demonstrate. Some, misleadingly phrased, questions may sound interested only in what you know. All answers will still need to show how much you have thought.

2 Researching an answer

Before you begin to think about the overall shape of your essay, you must gather information and ideas.

Read the whole of each set text

The absolute priority is to investigate any work which the essay title specifies as your subject. You must read every word of it. However long it is and however tedious some passages seem at first glance, there can be no skip-reading. If you find that you have been day-dreaming for a few pages, or even a few lines, go back and read them properly.

On some rare and regrettable occasions, other commitments or sheer incompetence in organizing your time may interfere. You may still not have read all the set texts thoroughly when you need to begin your essay if you are to meet the deadline. In such an event, do not start writing. Go to your tutor. Explain or confess. Plead for more time. You may not be popular; but you will cause far greater resentment by producing an essay on texts which you have not fully explored. To do so is a crass waste not only of your own efforts but also of your reader's.

READ AGAIN

Whenever possible, read a work more than once. If your entire essay is to be devoted to a single poem of less than a hundred lines, you must read it slowly and thoughtfully at least three times before you begin to plan an answer. If, by contrast, your essay must discuss a pair of long novels or plays, you will probably have to settle for reading each in its entirety just once. Even here, however, you should be selecting passages to which you intend to return. Find a few chapters in each novel or a few scenes in each play which strike you as crucial. Give these at least a second and ideally a third reading.

READING ALOUD

If you are reading verse, listen as well as look. Read as much as you can aloud. Alertness to specifics can be aroused by this method when you are studying many prose works too, and not just plays or novels that rely on dialogue.

When you are going to recite some passage out loud, think what pace or tone seems appropriate. Try to hear the voice prescribed by the printed page, to articulate its meaning loyally and to do justice to its emotive potential. Observe how often a passage exploits sound effects. The more it does so, the more necessary it will be to read it aloud if you are to notice what you are reading.

READ WITH YOUR DICTIONARY READILY AT HAND

You must possess a dictionary as an essential tool of the trade. Do not try to skip any word which you do not fully understand. Pause to explore the context. If that does not decisively reveal what the word must mean, consult your dictionary. The dictionary you own will be relatively small. It has to be easy to handle and not so expensive as to give your bank manager apoplexy. So in some cases it will be inadequate. Then jot down words which must be explored in some larger dictionary at the library.

Where you suspect an English word of having changed its meaning down the centuries, only the full, many-volumed version of the *Oxford English Dictionary* will do. It gives all the major meanings available to author and reader at all periods of literary history. Its definitions are supported by quotations from works published at each stage of a developing word's life. You can thus see how words were used in texts contemporary with the one which you are studying.

LEAVE EACH BOUT OF READING MEMORIZING A SPECIFIC

If you pause at the end of one act of a play or a chapter of a novel or one poem in a collection, do not close your mind as you close the book. While you are making a cup of coffee or putting on your coat to go out, recite to yourself a line or phrase from the text which you have just been reading. Each time, you should acquire some fragment of the text's own texture even if the extract is no more than three or four words long. What you have learnt by heart you can carry around in your head. Pondering, even in the oddest places, such unofficial acorns can often nurture them into intellectual oaks of extraordinary strength and complexity.

Make notes

Do not just start turning the pages of a specified text, hoping that insight will seep up through your fingertips. Read with pen in hand and a determination to make frequent notes. Unless you are constantly looking for points worth recording, you will discover few and remember less.

Some of your notes should be exposing such localized details that you may want to add underlines and marginalia to the relevant page of the printed text. Such annotations are unlikely to muffle the text's own chosen chronology since that remains visibly present among your own comments. When later you consult your running commentary you still have the appropriate passage of the text before you and can discover more than you had first registered. You may find it helpful also to compose your own index inside the back cover of a book, assembling references to all the contexts in which a particular character appears or some recurrent theme is explored or some crucial word is deployed. Of course, you may be among those who regard the marking of books as sacrilegious. Even if you are not, the copy that you are reading may not be your own but the library's or a friend's, and then there can be no question of adding even the most lightly pencilled comment.

Obviously you will anyway need to make fuller notes elsewhere. Design a system for these that concentrates your particular kind of mind and bully yourself into using it.

Do check, as your notes grow, that you are not just producing a paraphrase. The risk of this is greatest when you are handling a long work. You may be tempted, after reading another chapter of a novel and jotting down a summary of the main plot events that it contains, to stop writing and proceed immediately to read the next chapter. Such notes will prove almost useless when you come to write your essay. Of course, in some contexts, narrative structure can be a relevant, and indeed, fascinating issue; but to discuss it sensibly you will need to have noticed and remembered far more than simply the number of a chapter in which some incident occurs.

The most helpful entries in your notes will be those that record your own thoughts about the significance of the passage that your reading has then reached. Many of these will define issues which you cannot hope to resolve until, at the very least, you have read the entire text. Meanwhile, to read alertly means to read questioningly. You should begin to be suspicious if, as your notes grow, they are not including many suggestions that end in question marks.

Another danger sign is a steady consistency in the length of notes that each chapter of a novel or each scene of a play has inspired. This will almost certainly mean that you are not thinking hard enough to make even provisional decisions as to which parts of the text matter more than others, and which issues are so unusually complex that you need to use more words if you are to remember what you thought.

Worry, too, if notes on later portions of a long work do not include references to earlier ones. You cannot be thinking about the impact of what you are reading if you do not notice some emerging patterns of anticipation and echo, or some potentially interesting points of comparison and contrast, which your essay can eventually investigate.

Finally, do check that you are including verbatim quotations, however brief some of these may be. If you are being sufficiently alert to the ways in which style determines substance, you will find yourself recording examples to remind yourself of exactly what you did notice about the text's own use of language. The actual process of copying out extracts may jog you into registering more about their phrasing or their precise implications. Do accompany each quotation by a reminder as to why it strikes you as significant. Even if the reason now seems to you self-evident, do trouble to spell it out for the sake of your future self.

When you are reading a text for the first time, you will have to settle initially for a simple, chronological arrangement of notes following the text's own sequence of chapters or scenes or stanzas. In other cases you may choose to organize some, or even all, of your notes into separate sections on particular topics. If so, be sure that you do still notice the text's own choice of the order in which readers must meet its manipulative devices of language or its puzzles and revelations in thought and plot. Some of your headings could invite notes about, for instance, narrative structure. All of your entries should be accompanied by exact references. Fail to do this and you will not just underestimate the significance of the text's timing; you may also waste an infuriating amount of time later in finding some quotation whose accuracy you need to check.

Allow your growing experience of the text to correct or expand your sense of what the significant issues are. Expect to delete or rephrase some headings and to add many more. Even if you have not been asked simply to 'write an essay on' some named text but are faced by a far more specific question, do try to prevent its exerting an undue influence on what your notes discover in the text. Your first guesses as to what will prove relevant are likely to be too narrow. You anyway want to gain much more from your reading than just one essay. How you define your loftier or more hedonistic purposes will depend on your own view of the uses of literature. However, you will want these notes to have value long after you have written your essay. Ensure that their range and depth will still be an adequate resource when quite different issues are raised by an examiner or by your own maturing curiosity.

You may think it worth while to accumulate, at the same time as your full notes on the text, a separate and far more selective series of jottings in response to the demands of a set question. The inevitable duplication need not cost too much time and effort if you use sufficient cross-references from your essay notes to fully written-out quotations and ideas in your resource notes. Demarcation lines will often be hard to draw but any conscious difficulty here can be useful in forcing you, from the outset of your reading, to start thinking about what your essay should include to be a sufficiently thoughtful and detailed answer and what it may have to exclude if it is to define a clear sense of priorities. If you do decide to make separate essay notes, these must at first be highly provisional. No decisions about what subjects deserve whole paragraphs or how these should be ordered can be made until, at the very least, you have finished reading all the relevant texts.

Secondary sources and some problems in literary theory

Works of literary theory, history, biography or criticism are often called 'secondary' sources and distinguished from 'primary' ones which, for your purposes in writing an essay, are those literary texts specified as your subject and any other works of literature which seem to you essential comparisons. The terminology implies a hierarchy which you should probably accept since most teachers will insist that study of the primary texts must be your priority.

Nevertheless, the distinction between primary texts – supposedly original, autonomous works of art – and secondary sources – arguably parasitical since they admit to being texts about texts – can be misleading. A work which might traditionally have been called 'creative' literature may itself be highly derivative. It may critically reconstruct fragments from already extant texts so that a well-read audience can interpret this new arrangement in the light of earlier ones, and vice versa.

Conversely, the methods by which a critic manipulates language may be as creative in some senses as those deployed by, for instance, a novelist. Both may construct themselves as voices which the reader will trust to report accurately some pre-existent truth. The work of Donne described by T. S. Eliot in his essay on 'The Metaphysical poets' or the Dorset landscape described by Hardy in one of his novels are both perhaps newly created phenomena. Neither may have ever been seen in a reader's mind until they were given that precise verbal form.

Even if you decide to read a primary text like the Donne poem, and formulate your response to it, before reading T. S. Eliot's or anyone else's commentary on it, your interpretation and evaluation are likely to be already coloured by pressure from supposedly secondary sources. For instance, to make any kind of sense out of the more archaic or abstruse terminology in the poem, you may have to consult the notes in some scholarly edition. You then accept their author's choice of explanatory, modern words as part of the poem's meaning. Even those of the poem's own words which are most immediately meaningful to you will make sense only because you have met them in other contexts. In measuring the poem's worth, you are likely to be influenced by facts which derive, however indirectly, from views expressed in secondary sources. Is it likely that Donne would be on your syllabus at all if a powerful mass of critical commentary had not grown around his works since the 1920s? You might even have glimpsed a lecture list and deduced the relative importance Donne is given by those of your teachers who decide how many lectures should be devoted to each author.

Of course, you may be sturdily resilient when your own judgement is faced by such easily recognizable pressures. What, however, of the subtler ones: those implicit generalizations, pervading much of your literary education, as to what constitutes a great poem and how it should be interpreted? Your essay must, for instance, imply a view on whether early texts should be interpreted as their first readers may have understood them, or in the light of the modern reader's own values. Arguably, one of the main advantages of studying literature is that it reveals some of the utterly different assumptions made by even the most intelligent members of a past generation. It thus liberates us from an unquestioning acceptance of whatever value systems happen to operate in our own time and place. So learning more history is almost bound to make you a more interested – and interesting – reader of old texts.

Yet, even if you do decide that it is desirable to respond now as seventeenth-century readers once did, is it possible? There is the problem that those earlier readers disagreed on some issues so strongly that they quite often set about slaughtering each other. The modern reader cannot feel exactly like one of the passionately committed participants in such a dispute and at the same time maintain a balanced understanding of the factors that led both sides to see an issue so differently.

We learn about the past largely through reading texts written in our own time. These constructions of the past, composed by modern historians, cannot of course have influenced the seventeenth-century readers whose experience you may seek to recapture. Yet you cannot forget such constructions nor all the other more recent texts, whether literary or not, which have significantly shaped your own beliefs and feelings.

Moreover, partly under the influence of these texts, many of the verbal styles that seemed natural to at least some seventeenth-century readers have now come to sound quaintly old-fashioned. They have been replaced by new discourses reflecting the ideology of modern society. So the idioms in which we speak to each other or write literary criticism may force us to decode past verbalizations in a new way. However diligently you consult a glossary, old words will still sound old. However often you quote from an early text, your surrounding prose will still pose it in a context which would sound distinctly odd to its original readers.

Imagine that a group of suddenly resurrected Elizabethans appear round your desk while you are composing your next critical essay. As they begin to read over your shoulder, how much guidance would they need before they could begin to make sense of what you are doing? Remember that they come from a time when the vast majority of their fellow citizens had not been taught how to read anything at all, and that, for the educated few who could read and write, the texts which were thought most worth studying were in Latin or Ancient Greek. Your baffled visitors lived three centuries before some universities accepted the idea that texts written in one's own language could deserve serious study as literature. F. R. Leavis was among the first students on the Cambridge English Tripos, which, after a fairly ferocious controversy, was finally allowed to start in 1917. At about the same surprisingly late date, Cambridge at last decided that some women might be sufficiently intelligent to be allowed a chance at a university degree.

The fact that you are capable of writing some sort of critical essay and probably not capable of writing competent poetry in Latin, Ancient Greek and Italian (as Milton did) may have something to do with your own individual talents as an author. It most certainly has a lot to do with your education.

Moreover, your definitions of what kinds of knowledge or skill are worth acquiring do not derive only from your official teachers. You might try to list for yourself some of the innumerable other sources of influence which have determined what kind of statements seem to you worth making and what kind seem to you boring or meaningless.

Family and friends, books and magazines, films and television programmes, popular songs and advertisements are obvious influences; but think too of the structures within which you have met or made the various statements that you can understand and imitate. Would someone from the seventeenth century be able to grasp all those forces that determine the motivation and methodology which you will bring to writing your next critical essay? You would have to explain the modern system of further education and the demands it places upon the group of students to which you belong; the criteria for admission to particular institutions; the examination system; the rewards of academic success in terms of jobs, status and social mobility. Some of these issues might require you to sketch the overall political, economic and social system of the country.

You would have to explain that 'literature' no longer means (as it still did in the seventeenth century) the entire body of available books and other writings; that a tiny minority of texts are currently given an especially privileged status as literature; that this literature is divided on national lines; and that authorship, even in the case of theatre scripts, is now regarded as a crucial factor in the evaluation of literary works. Your visitors would need to be told that this process of evaluation has been a major growth area for over half a century and now provides full-time employment for some of the most sophisticated people in our society.

Think, too, of all the more specific advice that you would need to offer about the genre of a student essay in criticism before your time-travellers could begin to interpret your essay's content, let alone judge the quality of its style and structure. It may be that you, in spite of being its author, could not afford the time to explain much about your own feelings or your personal morality. There would be so many more obviously necessary explanations about the demands in which your essay originates.

Of course, there are important senses in which your essay should, and can, reflect your own opinions and responses, and other portions of this book are largely devoted to helping you to do just that. Nevertheless, you can use your own experience as a writer to see that even the most honest attempts at self-expression are shaped not only by the author but by the readers he or she anticipates. Think of the strikingly distinct prose-styles that you use in writing letters. The joky one to an old schoolfriend, where your syntax and vocabulary are designed to show that you still speak the same language, will obviously be quite different from the style in which you try to persuade either a stranger that you deserve a job, or a distant relative that you are grateful for a present. These are not differences of truth and falsehood. In all three cases you may feel that you can sincerely claim to have values in common with your correspondent. But to make that claim acceptable in each case demands a different authorial voice. Now consider the essay through which you prove that you do belong in the academic community by showing your familiarity with yet another set of linguistic and social conventions. This text will resemble in many ways those essays which other students on the same course are submitting. It may sound unrecognizably different from any of the letters which you, as a supposedly original author, have composed at much the same time.

Yet, if you are not thinking hard enough, you may imply, in this very essay, that texts always portray their authors' personalities rather than their anticipated readers' demands. You may even find yourself evaluating some novel on the premise that, if its characters are accurately drawn, their speech and behaviour will reflect their own autonomous personalities and not the rules of any social game which they are required to play.

The concept of personality dominates much of the literary criticism that you are likely to have so far read. Not only have texts been seen as originating in, and reflecting, their authors'

personalities. Their subject-matter and stance have been presented as favouring individual experience and the intimacies
of personal relationships. Their readers have been encouraged
to see themselves as relatively private beings, each responding
alone, as sensitively as possible, to meanings that supposedly
exist on the page and not in some larger world where the
influential context of the language itself is constantly developing, where opinions are changed, societies alter, and the
relative power of different groups shifts.

That larger, more communal, world, some critics would still
argue, is not properly the business of the literary critic. The
student of linguistics, or of the history of ideas, or of philos-
ophy, may properly concentrate on the ways in which language alters, or is altered by, our intellectual assumptions. The
political theorist, sociologist or professional historian may
legitimately focus on the way such assumptions create, or are
created by, the texts of a particular social group. The literary
critic, a traditionalist might insist, has a prior duty to the texts
themselves, to their intrinsic meanings and innate worth.
What light they may be able to throw on problems in other
disciplines must be of secondary importance. Indeed, there
may be a positive danger in the critic's discussing such problems even peripherally. Might it not lead to the imposition
upon a text of some politically partisan meaning, and is not the
critic bound to attempt impartiality, to discover respectfully
what the text itself is really saying?

The problem here may be that no wholly innocent reading of
a text is possible. To write your essay on the assumption that it
is could blind you to numerous factors which may compel you
actively to produce the meanings that you seem to be just
passively discovering.

A text's import and worth may be subject to constant re-
definition as the conditions in which it is read alter. To take a
fairly obvious example, Shakespeare's history plays were reinterpreted at the time of the Second World War when national
survival seemed to depend on acceptance of strong central
government, and on a conspiracy to ignore, if only temporarily, those conflicts of interest which had been making dom-
estic politics so vigorous. E. M. W. Tillyard's book on the
plays (*Shakespeare's History Plays*, London, 1944) and Olivier's
rousingly patriotic film interpretation of *Henry V* were not seen

as propaganda but merely as practical attempts to make interesting sense of old texts for a modern audience. It is extremely hard to recognize contemporary productions of literary texts as localized, temporary and manipulative adaptations. One of the advantages of studying the history of literary reputations and the critical rationales by which these have been promoted or challenged is that distance of time exposes the creativity which may be involved in all readings.

Many writers, of course, still work on the assumption that such problems are slight and should be overcome. The greatest texts supposedly encapsulate truths which are, and always will be, as relevant as when they were first defined. The finest authors are seen as having been transcendentally superior to the people among whom they lived. Largely unaffected by contemporary habits of thought and patterns of language, they discovered original meanings which they then crystallized into new verbalizations. Centuries later, unless we are too distracted by merely superficial aspects of modern life, we can still decode the author's intended message and see how it remains just as applicable today.

There is a paradox here. Is the text to be admired for its universality or its uniqueness? To the traditionalist critic, the author is essentially an individual, valued for rarity of vision and novelty of insight. Genius invents its own style, constructing a hitherto unavailable experience in a previously unknown pattern of signs. Yet, if the text is also to be valued for communicating recognizable truth, it may need to tell readers what they already know. Your essay may suggest that we can evaluate the accuracy of a landscape poet by remembering the literal appearances of the natural world itself; or that we can measure the subtlety of a novelist's characterization by comparing the fictional personages with our prior knowledge of how real people behave. The text's language has somehow to be the original creation of an extraordinary person and a precise echo of what many generations of ordinary readers have always believed.

The paradox may be explicable in terms of 'What oft was thought but ne'er so well expressed'. The implicit premise here is that reality exists quite independently from the vocabulary in which we may sometimes choose to describe it. The mind can supposedly look at the world, or experience its own movements, without recourse to words. It may or may not then decide to seek out verbal equivalents for what it has already understood.

Many modern critics now work on the contrary hypothesis. They suggest that it is language itself which allows us to form a view of human experience. We see things distinct from one another only because we have a vocabulary in which literally to tell them apart. In the beginning was not 'thought' but 'the word'. When a text proposes one construction of experience as peculiarly 'well expressed' we judge its claim by reference to other, equally verbal constructions through which we have hitherto shaped our thoughts.

What our language allows to sound sensible will seem true, and even our most private thoughts may derive – however unconsciously – from language. Perhaps we discover what sense we are making of things only by talking to ourselves and listening to the words in which we define our experience. If what our vocabulary cannot name remains literally unthinkable, language is the name of all the games which our minds can play.

Some modern theorists thus advance serious reasons for approaching literature playfully. A text should be prevented from persuading us that it can refer to some reality beyond language. When Burns assures us that his girl-friend is 'like a red, red rose/That's newly sprung in June', we should perhaps notice how often we have 'read, read' this way of talking about women in the highly sexist discourse of our love-poetry.

Most of the distinctions between men and women that we take for granted have been written in by our language. Where other languages draw different lines between the genders, love functions differently. For instance, in a society where physically demanding labour with crops and livestock is re-garded as women's work, cultural tradition may more often have celebrated a beloved girl's body for its functional strength and less often for its decorative delicacy.

The Burns poem also relies upon our language's hierarchical ability to tell the difference between flowers and weeds. In a vocabulary which grouped vegetation according to edibility rather than appearance, roses might provide less flattering similes. If we turn a deaf ear to the reminder that a rose's value depends on our having been taught to read, we may mistake for a law of nature what is only one transient and tendentious way of speaking. Texts perhaps tell us not what human nature or the natural world are really like but how one group in a society at just one point in its developing history has constructed these ideas.

In saying that it is 'My love' that is 'like a red, red rose', the poem is ambiguous: 'love' may mean either the abstract feeling of desire and affection or the concrete person who is beloved. Yet 'My' ensures that either of these loves must be seen as the personal property of a voice which is firmly singular, possessive and – because we know our way around our own culture – presumably male. What it owns and apprehends is a visible beauty that exists only when 'newly sprung in June' and will, by implication, soon fade.

Male readers may feel moved here by a poignant suggestion that female beauty – which they seek to possess and retain – all too quickly disappears. A feminist reader, if she, too, takes 'My love' to mean the poet's girl-friend, is not likely to admire the text's implication that adolescent girls do briefly fascinate but all too soon mature into irrelevance. She may feel able to evaluate the poem more highly if she interprets 'My Love' as referring to the poet's own emotion: like all constructions of feeling – including all those ways in which women have been read – it will eventually be dismantled.

The traditional critic might protest that the pun on red/read is impertinently creative; that the reader's task is to receive in humble passivity the meaning which the text imposes: the poem tells us clearly enough how it wishes to be interpreted here. Yet, to produce even the conventional reading, we need to know far more than the poem's own words. It is our experience of countless other texts which prevents us assuming that Burns must fancy women with scarlet skin or enjoy cutting off their legs and sticking them in vases.

Some student essays – and not necessarily the worst – still concentrate exclusively on internal evidence from the primary text and resolutely ignore the existence of any secondary sources which may have determined its origins, its initial reception and its current reputation. In so doing, whether they recognize what they are up to or not, they imply their support for one theory of how literature should be read, and their rejection of many others. If, on the other hand, you do design a pattern of secondary sources as an illuminating context in which to appreciate the primary text, your choice and presentation of supporting material will obviously reveal your principles. So do use some of your reading time for essays in literary theory. Curiosity about what you are trying to achieve in writing criticism must increase your chances of success. Moreover, even those students who feel intimidated by the prospect of studying literary theory usually find in practice that discovering a wider range of approaches can be fun.

Literary history and biography

A firm line is often drawn between scholarship as facts and criticism as opinions. The information offered by a competent literary historian or biographer is supposedly true even if of debatable relevance. By contrast, criticism, the argument runs, admits to making only partial and partisan contributions to a continuing debate; so you should read it critically, feeling sceptical and even downright suspicious about what it wishes you to believe.

Yet even a textual editor, whom you at first take to be fastidiously neutral and motivated solely by a wish to give you the exact words of the text as its author intended, has to make choices. The most elaborate variorum edition may still demote some versions to a lowly and ghostly existence at the foot of the page while privileging others above in a larger print as if these form the only true text. Certainly some commentators would now argue that literary history, like all history, is inevitably partisan. Its author may never explicitly define – let alone rationally defend – any theoretical premises. Yet limited space will force selectivity. Many authors and texts will not be openly attacked but just silently condemned as not even deserving to be mentioned. The few that are judged admissible will be related to each other in a patterned sequence: some systems of connection and distinction will be given priority; others will be quietly rejected. An implicit hierarchy of values will also emerge in the varying amounts of space awarded to different texts. More specifically, what aspects of any one text are foregrounded and which ways of reading it are recommended will depend on the expert's own convictions as to what a culture should create or conserve.

The converse process by which certain emphases and inter-pretations are censored is potentially even more costly. Of course, a politically radical interpretation of *Paradise Lost* or *The Prelude* need not be explicitly forbidden as wickedly subvers-ive. The scholar's approach can just bypass it as ignorantly tangential: a cul-de-sac fit only for the ill-informed or the simple-minded. The English Civil War may be briefly acknowl-edged as contemporary with Milton's epic. The French Rev-olution may be mentioned as close in time to Wordsworth's verse autobiography. Yet, in a guide to the origins of *Paradise Lost*, Virgil and Dante might still be given overwhelmingly more space than contemporary politics. An account of how *The Prelude* discovered its substance and style may devote far more pages to Wordsworth's study of earlier poets (particularly Milton himself, as it happens) than to his experience of revol-ution in Paris or his later fears that England itself might become unrecognizably democratic.

Literary history can in fact reduce itself to a mere history of literature, as if the history of classes and nations had de-veloped in some wholly separate world. The influence of author upon author may leave little room for the effect of major events upon texts. It may leave none at all for the production or prevention of major events by texts themselves.

You may think that texts simply do not have that kind of power; you may think that they mirror, rather than create, the beliefs which determine behaviour. Certainly, to seem com-prehensible to their contemporary readers, texts do have to work within a given vocabulary. The parameters of that vo-cabulary do perhaps reflect the prevailing political climate. A text's language must acknowledge those distinctions between the meaningfully important and the meaninglessly trivial which are accepted by the dominant culture. Nevertheless, within these limits, an energetic work of literature may still make itself sufficient room for manoeuvre to redefine its readers' assumptions about what is conceivable or desirable. 'Poets', as Shelley argues in his preface to *Prometheus Unbound*, 'are in one sense the creations and in another the creators of their age'.

So, too, are scholars and critics. Their preferences among

texts can be both cause and effect of what modern society values in its past history. Shelley himself, for instance, wrote a poem called 'England in 1819' about a major political event of that year. Unarmed and peaceful demonstrators in Manchester had been listening to speeches in favour of ordinary people being allowed the vote. Cavalry with drawn sabres were sent in to disperse them. Many men and women were injured. Some were killed. Shelley in that year wrote more than one poem which might have made the massacre an unforgettable martyrdom to be remembered by any reader who values freedom. The poems, like those whom they seek to commemorate, are in fact now largely forgotten. Yet as an attentive student of literary history, you may still learn to remember 1819 as a crucial year because it was then that Keats wrote odes to a nightingale and to a piece of ancient Greek pottery.

Literary biography can be as tendentious as literary history. Sentimental concentration upon Milton's physiological blindness or gossip about his personal difficulties in relating to women are obviously distractions from the poetic texts. But even the most sophisticated literary biographies encourage certain responses to the text and discourage others. By definition of genre, such biography implies that a text's author is a major issue; that discovering what a writer intended in composing a text is possible and indeed profitable; that the author's own interpretation and even evaluation may legitimately determine ours.

Moreover, personalizing a text as the product of some interestingly individualistic intellect often leads to its content being structured around other supposed individuals. A novel's characterization may be assumed to matter more than its support for, or challenge to, the values of a given society. If a playwright's own idiosyncrasies of behaviour are emphasized, then the voices of the dramatic text are likely to be explored as interestingly deviant from, rather than typical of, a particular social group or economic class.

The alliance of literary historians and biographers can be exemplified by the reported superiority of Elizabethan to medieval drama. *Dr Faustus* is often described as an advance on *Everyman* less because it offers a subtler analysis of its society than because it explores the idiosyncratic thoughts and feelings of its individualistic characters. You are likely to be reminded – however discreetly – by scholars recommending this hierarchy that *Everyman* is anonymous whereas *Dr Faustus* was written by Kit Marlowe about whose life we know a few racy stories.

I am only suggesting that you should read historical and biographical works critically – not that you should ignore them. For many of the tasks undertaken early in a literary apprenticeship, some mapping of the available texts and of the ways in which they can be related is absolutely essential, and learning about an author's life may well stimulate you into returning to the works with renewed curiosity. Moreover, an intelligent biographer will offer you a portrait of the society which formed the author's so-called personality, and explain what assumptions in the original readership the texts had to anticipate. The language of the work that you mean to appreciate is arguably the language of a particular tribe at one time in its history. Of course, if you believe in genius and its magically transforming power, you may want to concentrate upon the originality with which a gifted author deploys that vocabulary. Even this, however, requires some knowledge of what all members of a given social group once defined as sensible or senseless. Only those who have learnt to speak a common language can measure the extent to which some texts put it to uncommon use.

Published criticism

Some students find that the wider their wanderings among the critics the more they can discover in the text itself. They return to the text alerted to the range of ways in which it can be enjoyed and curious about their own sense of priorities. It helps them in fact to read more thoughtfully and observantly.

Others find published criticism distracting or inhibiting. They tend to be overwhelmed by memories of someone else's emphases. They feel nervous about their own interest in issues which published critics have ignored. They may even find that they have simply spent so much time reading critical articles that they have too little left to gain a confident knowledge of the text itself.

Provided that you explore other people's opinions to stimulate yourself into discovering and defining your own, reading published criticism is bound to improve your essays. But so many students seem to have difficulty in nerving themselves to criticize the critics that it seems worth risking a few simple rules.

Get into the habit of reading reviews of new books of literary criticism in *The Times Literary Supplement* and similar journals. Here you will sometimes find critics being accused by each other, not just of being mistaken, but of having produced uselessly irrelevant or dangerously misleading books. Observing how often those in the trade fear that the customer is being conned should prevent your approaching the library shelves with undue reverence.

Do ask your teachers – and your fellow students – about published essays they have found useful. Encourage them to remember which specific aspects of a text or topic seemed to be illuminated by a given book or article.

Always read more than one critic's account of any primary text that you are investigating. Notice where the critics disagree: not just in their more explicit conclusions but in less obvious ways too. Notice, for instance, the different parts of the text that each selects as worth any consideration at all. Try to spot any premises about literature or life which one seems to assume with more confidence than the other. Noticing where they differ from each other should help you to define where your views disagree with theirs.

Notice also what critics have in common. Do take an interest in when a piece of criticism was first published. Try to observe how fashions for certain kinds of approach have occurred at certain stages.

There is, of course, no guarantee that criticism in any ultimate sense makes progress. So beware of patronizing works that you discover were written long ago. On the other hand, do always try to find some articles which have been written recently and which your hard-pressed tutor may not find too familiar. The Modern Language Association publishes annual bibliographies of literary criticism. If you have access to a major library that stocks these and most of the journals where listed articles appeared, do use it. Even if your facilities are more limited, try to find some essays published in the last ten or perhaps fifteen years. It is obviously absurd, now that we are coming so close to the twenty-first century, vaguely to take anything written since 1900 as equally 'modern'.

Try to approach a published essay of criticism not just as a set of opinions which could equally well be paraphrased, but as a carefully composed exercise in rhetoric. Observe how its prose-style claims a given personality for its author and constructs one for its reader. There are, for instance, critics who make assumptions about the social class and even the gender of the people who will read their essays. Notice, too, the relative weighting of different stages of the argument and the sequence in which these have been arranged. Observing techniques of style and structure will save you from mistaking one person's effort for the word of God. It should also give you useful tips as to how you can make your own criticism more persuasive or amusing.

Sample only a few pages of a critical essay and then make a decision as to whether it will prove useful. In some cases, just a few paragraphs may convince you that the author's topic or approach is too remote from your own and that you must move on to try another essay if you are to find enough genuinely thought-provoking material in the time available.

On those that do prove worth reading in full, you must make notes or you will soon forget what you have learnt. Do not just write down a paraphrase of, or quotations from, the critic's views. Record, too, as frequently as possible, your own reactions. Reservations – including reference to any textual evidence that the critic seems to be forgetting or undervaluing – may prove particularly useful. Record your observations not only of what is argued but also of how that argument is presented.

But what you will value most highly afterwards is your record of your own new ideas which have just been stimulated by your reading. Make sure that you identify unmistakably the precise point at which your summary of the critic gives way to your own thoughts, and that at which your observations about the text cease and a summary of the critic's begins once more. Use a system of square brackets or separate columns or different coloured inks: anything provided that it is absolutely clear. Your notes must remind you of what is, and is not, your own to avoid any risk of accidental plagiarism in your essay. There is anyway a more immediate gain: you can see by a glance at your notes whether the published essay is provoking you to many noteworthy thoughts of your own or is producing no more than an uninterrupted summary of its own propositions. If long uninterrupted, they are almost certainly being accepted unquestioningly. Wake up and start thinking. Alternatively, decide that this piece of criticism is not capable of interesting you into thinking for yourself and abandon it. Try another instead.

For every critical book or article that your notes summarize or quote, a full reference – author, title, date, publisher and page numbers – must be included. Your essay's bibliography will need to give most of this information, and on various future occasions, you may need to refer quickly to some passage which your notes cite.

Discuss your essay subject with friends or relatives

Students too often work alone. Lonely minds get lazy, lose concentration, feel bored. So talk about the literary problems which you are tackling. Listen to other people's understanding of them. Discuss their proposed solutions. Informal teamwork can often make progress where the isolated intellect is stationary or fruitlessly circling.

If you explain to someone else what you think about a book, you will have a far clearer grasp of your own thoughts. If you listen to other people chatting about what they have noticed in a text or how they respond to some feature of it, you are almost bound to gain new ways of reading, thinking and eventually writing.

Of course, the person you like talking to most may know little or nothing about the relevant text. Yet discussion could still help you. Show someone a particular passage which fascinates or puzzles you. Even on the basis of only the haziest understanding of the overall context, he or she may notice specifics which you have missed, and may query premises which you have unconsciously taken for granted.

Where friends fail, and you are living with parents or spouse or reasonably mature siblings or offspring, try one of these. Some relative must like you enough to be interested in your interests. Explain where you need help in deciding what you think of a book or how best to design an answer to your essay's question. Spell out your feelings of pleasure or bafflement or anger at what a text seems to be doing and saying. Discover whether others understand your response, and do your best to understand theirs.

If at a late stage of preparing for a particular essay you still feel you have nothing to say which could interest a friend or relative, start worrying. Perhaps you have still not bullied yourself into finding sufficiently interesting ideas. Then you must be at risk of perpetrating the offence of producing an essay which merely states the drearily obvious. Perhaps, even though you are full of latently entertaining thoughts, you are still so vague about them that you cannot verbalize them adequately. If so, you are far from being ready to write your essay. What you cannot yet explain to someone who knows you well will make no sense to your tutor.

The grimmest explanation would be that you yourself are not sufficiently interested in how literature works to enjoy discussing it in your free time. In that case you should transfer to a different course. Find some subject about which you can care enough to think hard and do well.

If, on the other hand, literary texts are what you want to understand and yet you are still trying to make sense of them alone, you must be mismanaging your social life. Change it. Just possibly you should be trying to make new contacts but it is far more likely that you merely need to nerve yourself to make better use of your present ones. Work out what fear is inhibiting you and overcome it. Remember that others too may be hiding their own fears of being thought foolish or ignorant or over-earnest or simply interfering. Help them to help you. You are unlikely to write well about literature unless you can hear how you and others talk about it.

3 Planning an argument

A critical essay should not just express an opinion. It must advance an argument.

Often you will have been offered by a title – or discovered in your research – some crucial proposition on which you can centre the entire structure of your essay, examining the relevance and accuracy of that one claim. Your essay may eventually come to a concluding sentence which says little more than 'Yes, I do agree' or 'No, I do not'. Which of these destinations you choose to reach, though it should concern you, may not matter much to your reader. The route, however, certainly will.

Notice the sleeping metaphors of a journey in clauses like 'advancing an argument', 'exploring an issue', 'arriving at a judgement'. You should conduct your reader along a carefully planned path. The route must take in all the most interesting points and yet maintain an overall sense of direction. Good essays make progress.

Sensible essay-writers, like all competent guides, are properly equipped before they embark. They have clear priorities, and have allocated the time available to the different landmarks so that the more puzzling can be adequately explained, and the most interesting sufficiently explored. They have chosen the order in which these points will be reached, and the linking passages which can best connect them into a demonstrably logical itinerary. They also, of course, know the conclusion to which they will finally lead the reader; but they remember that to travel illuminatingly is more important than to arrive.

These strategic issues must all have been examined and resolved before you set out upon your first sentence. There you will be accompanied by your reader who will already be expecting guidance as to what is worth noticing and why. You must have a plan.

All critics do, of course, discover more about the text and their own thoughts as they write. While you are striving to find the best words with which to explain one point, you will often be alerted to some new idea. Then you may quite rightly decide to adapt your original structure so that your latest thoughts can be included. However, the more thought provoking you find the actual process of writing, the more essential it is to have already committed yourself to an overall design. You can then see whether what has just occurred to you does belong in the paragraph which you then happen to be writing. It may belong in a much earlier or later one. It may even deserve a paragraph to itself. If so, you must have a planned sequence so that you can see where the new paragraph can most logically be inserted.

Before you begin to compose any part of your essay, write out in note form the main points you mean to make. Add cross-references to relevant passages in your full notes: to passages that offer more detailed evidence with which to define and support each proposition or those which offer more extended summaries of the arguments involved. Revise your ordering of your main points until you are satisfied that you have found the most illuminating and persuasive sequence in which to lead your reader through them.

If this process proves so difficult that it threatens to consume a great deal of time, ask yourself whether you are ready to design a plan and to write your essay. It may be that you still need to do more reading, thinking and note taking.

Throughout that earlier stage of researching an answer, you should have been wondering how many issues your essay can explore, and how they relate to each other. As your reading led you to ask one question, you will have been trying to see whether an answer to it must depend on other problems which need to be resolved first. Conversely, you will have been wondering, once you have decided on how a given issue should be resolved, whether that answer in itself provokes other questions. You will also have been curious, as more and more topics and ideas occur to you, as to whether each one will, in the last resort, matter more or less than others. So, by the time you come to write out a plan, many of the relevant policies should already have emerged, and only need to be recorded in a sufficiently centralized and economical format.

Writing out such a summary should certainly clarify your scale of priorities and may usefully trigger some additional ideas. However, its main use at this stage is to allow you to see all the insights and arguments that you have produced earlier, and to order them into a suitable structure.

Your plan will, of course, codify the distinguishable topics that you mean to investigate, and outline the kinds of information that you intend to deploy. You obviously need to be clear about what and how much you can probe in the available space. You do need to commit yourself to sounding well-informed, which here will usually mean sounding well-read. However, not all those who are well-read read well. So your plan must also commit your essay to sounding thoughtful. Check that it does not just list subjects but also summarizes your opinions. Where it notes passages of the text that you intend to cite, make sure there is some note as to the significance you intend to claim for them. Anticipate a reader who, whenever you observe some specific feature of a work, will ask 'So what?'. The propositions that your essay will advance need to be spelt out in the bald note form of your plan. Then you can seize this last chance to check that they do reflect your own beliefs or, at the very least, that they still seem to you both tenable and interesting.

Narrowing the scope

You may find that your first version of a plan is committing your essay to attempting more of the available tasks than can be performed well in the space available. Many essay titles do ask too much. They allude to so much literature in such vague terms that an answer could grow to book length without disgressing. You will often have to limit the range of your own relatively brief essay.

This process of selection will, of course, have been in your mind from the moment that you first began to read and make notes. Now you must make your final decisions, and some may seem bitterly wasteful. Whole areas of debate which you have pondered may have to be excluded. Whole texts on which you had made notes may, after all, have to remain unmentioned. A large idea or localized observation which had seemed to you so innately interesting that you looked forward to including it in your essay may turn out to be irrelevant to your planned argument and have to be discarded.

The relationship between this selection of your material and your strategy for arranging and ordering it needs to be flexibly reciprocal. If you find that many of your favourite quotations or shrewdest comments are having to be excluded because your intended structure provides no logical place for them, ask yourself whether your plan is right. Perhaps it should be adapted or expanded.

Remember, however, that a shapeless holdall, however generously packed with bright ideas and interesting quotations, will confuse and bore your reader. If you try to mention too many works, or even too many specific portions of one relatively long work, you may find that there is space only to mention them. That, of course, is useless. The mere assertion that you have read, however hastily, thirty relevant poems will not impress. The demonstration that you have thoroughly explored three will.

Be ruthless. What your essay has room to discuss must be decided rationally now. It must not be randomly imposed later by your simply discovering that you have run out of space and time in which to go on writing.

Weighing the proportions

Some titles and topics may require you to tackle so many different texts and distinguishable techniques that the need for selection has been self-evident from the outset and you have produced a plan which lists your chosen items. You may still have problems in deciding how much space each should be allowed.

You might, for instance, be tackling this: 'Do Donne's secular and religious poems employ similar techniques?' Your plan's list of texts might contain a dozen titles: five religious poems, five secular poems and a couple which you think are interesting as marginal cases which could be interpreted as belonging in either group.

You will not have space to treat all these with equal thoroughness. Whatever your view may be on the title's overall question of comparison, you will need at some stage to offer sustained and detailed accounts of a few whole poems. Obviously you must not allow your argument to fragment into a mere anthology of midget essays each of which offers a self-contained analysis of one poem. Yet some of your paragraphs must concentrate on the interaction of different techniques within a single work.

Do you devote one such paragraph to each poem or should you deal with even fewer works but give each a more extended discussion of two or even three paragraphs? The merits of range have to be weighed against the advantages of depth. You might explore the cumulative impact of all the techniques used within each work and go into so much detail that you can give only a full account of one religious and one secular poem. That would probably be excessive. On the other hand, readings of as many as a dozen poems would have to be confined to twelve vulnerably brief paragraphs. These could show no more than a superficial grasp of each work's shifting style and developing implication.

The choice will, of course, depend on how many paragraphs need to be reserved for other purposes. Presumably you will also want to have some paragraphs which can show how a particular technique remains recognizable throughout the various poems which deploy it, however varying its immediate context and localized connotation. If one seems to you demonstrably crucial, and if you do have permission to write a relatively long essay, you might allow two, or even three, consecutive paragraphs to explain how, and how well, the texts use that particular method. You may, however, have to confine yourself to writing one paragraph each even on those few techniques that interest you most. For the others, you may have to find some logical groupings which will justify your considering two or three together within a single paragraph.

Your larger ideas on the essay question will also need to be assessed. Which deserve most and which least space? Which will strike your reader as relatively fresh? Which, however promisingly unfamiliar they may be, are sufficiently straight-forward to be explained briefly, and which are so marginally relevant that they merit only a sentence each? Which are so complex or controversial that they will need to be accompanied by a great deal of detailed evidence to make them clear and convincing?

Some paragraphs might need to be reserved for principles. The premises which will only be implicit in more specific passages may need to be more openly debated and defended. On this Donne question, for instance, you might wish to gather together your thoughts about the difficulties of defining 'religious'. Can this be done in a couple of sentences of the opening paragraph or will it need a whole paragraph to itself?

Moreover, this set question about similarity of techniques may strike you as frustratingly tangential to the comparisons that you find most interesting between Donne's secular and religious verse. You may need to allow space for arguing that the issues which seem to you more certainly important are in fact inseparable from those explicitly specified by the title.

There is no right or wrong answer to the question of how many texts or topics should receive sustained treatment and how many must be discussed more briefly. The thoughtful critic is simply the one who sees the problem at the planning stage, and chooses a strategy which is defensible as the least of available evils.

Paragraphing

Each of your paragraphs must of course be centred on a particular issue which is raised by the set title. Each paragraph must be recognizable as a logical next step in a coherently developing argument that directly answers the set question. Nevertheless, in debating the value of including a particular paragraph, you should also ask yourself the following questions:

1) Will this paragraph prove that I have read one or more specific texts which are demonstrably relevant?
2) Will it show that I have read observantly? Will it contain specifics which only an attentive reader would have noticed?

3) Will it explain clearly that I have thought about the precise implications of what I have read and their effect upon my judgement of the major set text(s)?

If you doubt its ability to perform all these tasks, at least consider cutting the paragraph on the grounds that it might dilute your answer.

You may think that these three questions conspire to enforce a limiting emphasis on close reading of particular texts. What of the larger issues about literature, and indeed society, which many essay topics raise, if only implicitly? An essay for a Critical Theory course, for instance, may need to risk a paragraph which does not even name a single work of literature or criticism, let alone demonstrate any close knowledge of its localized effects. Specific examples may indeed overemphasize the exceptional, and evade important and interesting questions about what all texts in a particular genre or written at a particular time have in common. Close reading may allow too little space for curiosity about the processes at work when any text is being read. Even on these larger issues, my own prejudice would be to hope for clarifying examples. Nevertheless you – or your teacher – may think that trio of questions is too constricting. If so, you could usefully try to compose one or more extra questions to represent other demands which you think an acceptable paragraph might fulfil.

The essential is to be clear as to what each paragraph is meant to discuss and to make sure, by clear labelling in your plan, that all the relevant material will be assembled within it. It is no use vaguely noting 'paragraphs 3–5: Defoe's style'. That will just lead to an amorphous mass of observation and ideas. You will begin each new paragraph only because the preceding one looks rather long. So specify. Identify three distinct features which justify your three separate paragraphs:

Paragraph 3: unpretentious, familiar diction
Paragraph 4: straightforward syntax/short sentences
Paragraph 5: frequent listing of objects & calculations of amount – accounting-book prose.

Your essay plan should go into sufficient detail to save you from false strategies in good time. For instance, you may decide that you have, after all, so few interesting points to make about vocabulary and syntax that they should become a single paragraph labelled 'simplicity'. Conversely you might now recognize that the material intended for paragraph 5 is in fact so thought provoking that it can usefully be expanded and divided into two paragraphs: one now labelled 'concrete detail, lists of objects, descriptions of physical gestures and clothes', and another summarized in 'recurrent fascination with economic terms, literal calculations of cash in hand or in prospect and metaphorical use of "profit" and "loss" etc.'.

Each paragraph must not only have a clearly identified topic. It must also advance at least one major idea. Check that you now understand – and will later, when writing your essay, be able to explain – the precise relevance of each paragraph. Ask not only 'What is this paragraph to be about?' but also 'What am I going to say here and what will that prove in answer to the title's specified question?' Being clear about how each point supports your overall argument will often show you where it must be positioned for maximal effect.

As you begin to make provisional decisions about which paragraphs belong together, check that in a pair which you intend to make adjacent each does make a clearly distinct point. Points may deserve separate paragraphs because they concern different, if related, issues:

Paragraph (a): the portrayal of God in *Paradise Lost*
Paragraph (b): the portrayal of Satan in *Paradise Lost*.

These characters are active opponents in the work's narrative structure and direct contrasts in its dramatized ideology. They are thus sufficiently distinct and yet so mutually defining as to deserve separate but adjacent paragraphs.

Conflicting views of the same issue can deserve separate paragraphs too:

Paragraph (a): the case against the text: it fails to make God impressive and Satan suspect
Paragraph (b): the case for the text's success in ensuring the reader's respect for God and distaste for Satan
Paragraph (c): the moments at which *Paradise Lost* arguably succeeds because of, rather than in spite of, its failure to justify God and discredit Satan.

Notice here that a latently static see-sawing between opposed views of the same topic is only allowed to last for two paragraphs. The third usefully advances to a new possibility. In dividing and ordering paragraphs remember that critical arguments move forward. Your plan must allow your essay to progress.

You may have an adequately long list of clearly distinct paragraphs, but find no guidance in the title as to how you should order them. You may have been simply told to 'Write an essay on Blake' or to 'Discuss the aims and achievements of Browning' or to 'Give an account of Byron's intellectual and moral concerns' or to 'Show the variety of Herbert's poetic techniques'. With luck and effort, the note-taking process may have alerted you to a central controversy around which you can order your individual paragraphs as a coherent debate. Alternatively, your own convictions may lead you to link a whole series of localized propositions into a single, developing argument. If neither of these strategies has emerged, you are at risk. You may be about to blunder into a list-like sequence of unrelated paragraphs. Each may begin with an implicit confession of its own arbitrary positioning and your essay's shapelessness:

Another interesting aspect of Blake's verse is. . . .
Browning also had other purposes. For instance, he aimed to. . . .
Other poems of Byron are about a very different subject. . . .
An equally common feature of Herbert's style consists of. . . .
One further poem deserves analysis. . . .

Instead of constructing an overall argument, the authors of such sentences just assemble a random run of self-contained, miniaturized essays.

You will usually be able to see that some paragraphs might be grouped together as aspects of the same broad topic. But thinking in terms of vaguely defined large divisions can do more harm than good. It provides the false security of thinking you have planned an argument when you have actually done nothing more intellectually strenuous than would be required if you had been asked to slice a cake. You may, at worst, think in terms only of the first half of your essay and the second. You might lump all your paragraphs about Browning's apparent 'aims' together without any attempt to find a logical order in which the distinguishable purposes can best be explained. You would then make the brilliant deduction that you need another block of paragraphs which are roughly about Browning's 'achievements'.

To turn mere grouping into persuasively logical argument, try to rephrase your noted heading for each group of paragraphs so that an inert description of subject is enlivened into an assertion of opinion. If, for instance, your essay plan for Herbert's style lists a group of paragraphs under the heading of 'imagery', substitute some simple proposition like 'Imagery is Herbert's greatest strength' or 'Herbert's imagery humanizes God'. Then try to redefine the topic of each component paragraph so that it can itself function more vigorously as an argument. Work out which of these more localized propositions needs to be established before some other can be logically advanced as now provenly relevant and tenable. You should finally be able to do much the same in reviewing the relationship of the groups themselves and in deciding which of these needs to be offered to the reader first.

Ideally, each group, like each of its component paragraphs, should be a necessary prerequisite of the next. By establishing one point you earn the right to proceed immediately to the next.

Systems for sequence

The most effective order will almost always emerge through thought about the particular problems which have occurred to you during your research on each essay's specific topic. If, however, you cannot think of an appropriate structure, some version of one of the following systems may serve. Be sure to adapt it thoughtfully both to the precise demands of any set question and to your own judgement as to what criticism should seek to achieve.

THESIS, ANTITHESIS, SYNTHESIS

Sometimes your essay can be ordered into a debate between two potentially accurate readings. You can consider the case for and against an author or text whose importance is disputable. You can investigate the evidence for two rival interpretations. You can weigh the relative advantages of two divergent approaches to see whether, for instance, an evaluative or historical analysis is most helpful in what it reveals and least costly in what it suppresses.

A judicious weighing of the arguments on both sides will usually lead to some new way of defining their relationship. Instead of a simplistic choice between mutually exclusive opposites you may at least be able to recommend a balanced view which can combine the most illuminating aspects of both ideas. At best you may be able to construct a quite distinct, third notion which redefines both the initial alternatives as misleading.

An answer which conducts a debate should not simply divide into two halves where a single proposition is defended remorselessly until a midway switch to equally consistent attack. The case for and the case against should recur often enough to ensure that your reader remains aware of both possibilities. On the other hand, if they alternate too rapidly each point will be made so briefly before giving way to some counter-argument that it will sound superficial.

One compromise is to subdivide an essay into three or four sections each of which offers its own thesis/antithesis/synthesis pattern. You deploy this pattern for each section of an argument rather than just once for the essay as a whole. You might have been asked, for instance, to 'Discuss whether Dickens is ultimately a serious or a comic novelist'. You might subdivide your answer into analyses of three texts. On each you could first consider the case for that novel's being read seriously in order either to appreciate its intellectual complexity or to identify its ideological stance. Then you could consider what it offers the reader's sense of humour. Thirdly, you could consider the possibility that some of its most thought-provoking incidents or descriptions or characters are also its most amusing. How coherent a synthesis does the text itself concoct out of its graver and lighter subjects or techniques? This tripartite pattern could then be repeated in discussing each of the remaining novels.

The same Dickens question could, of course, be answered in paragraphs about particular topics rather than whole texts.

These might discuss the more or less lighthearted aspects of characterization, style, plot, scene and setting, theme and stance, considering examples of each issue through a number of novels. Here, too, thesis and antithesis could shape various sections. One section might first discuss Dickens's most committedly amusing characters or the funnier components in his more ambiguous portraits. This evidence could then be balanced by characterization which seems designed to evoke poignancy or to articulate protest. A subsequent section could explore the verbal devices which are closest to casual, localized jokes and then those which contribute to a more sustained and thoughtful portrait of individual experience or social pressure.

If you are weighing so many controversial issues, the desirability of regular attempts at synthesis is uncertain. To follow the pros and cons in each case with a summary which merely reiterates some already established balance is useless. Do not indulge in: 'Thus it can be seen that sometimes Dickens chooses a setting because of its potential for humour and sometimes because landscape or architecture can be used for serious, symbolic purposes.' Such a method will merely impose a whole series of flaccidly vague conclusions throughout your essay. The final paragraph's inherent risk of imposing just one is quite sufficient.

But there may be ways here, too, of relating previously opposed views in some less obviously polarized way. For instance, a simple contrast between entertainingly hyperbolic caricatures and touchingly credible characters might be followed by a consideration of the way in which the plot compels the two groups to interact. You might wish to argue that the text often makes us laugh at the muddled way in which people speak only so that we are alerted to the dangerously confused definitions upon which they will act.

A merely summarizing synthesis is not worth a sentence. You should rely upon your detailed arguments to have implicitly made clear where the balance of probability lies. But a complicating synthesis which establishes some new relationship between thesis and antithesis can maintain progress and may be worth a whole paragraph.

PROPOSITION AND PROOF

You may believe so strongly in some thesis about how an author or work should be read that you cannot argue the antithesis with any honesty. The unconvinced sound unconvincing; so sometimes both integrity and expediency may require you to plead for one side throughout your essay. The opposition must of course be demonstrably considered; however, you perhaps regard its arguments as so feeble that you cannot devote to them an equal share of your essay. To do so might waste too much effort on mere demolition work, and you may think that constructive criticism is most helpful to you and your reader. It will usually be the texts, and not misleading or irrelevant accounts of them, that your essay means to expose.

Any assertion which you have found in the title and which seems to you overwhelmingly true can form the backbone of your essay. So can any view which you yourself have defined in researching an answer. Whatever its origins, you must redefine and complicate the proposition that you intend to support. Your structure must separate it into a number of more specific possibilities. One of these should have been offered before the end of your first paragraph. Establish its exact implications, its relevance and its credibility. Then use it to raise the next possibility and set about confirming that.

Ask yourself in each case: would this paragraph make any less sense, or be any less persuasive, if its argument did not follow the point made in the previous paragraph? Does the previous paragraph establish a view which I need the reader to have understood and conceded before I can explain and prove my present claim? If the answer is 'No', try again.

The danger is that you will just keep proving the same limited point by different means. Instead of a progressive argument, you settle into the stasis of an arbitrarily ordered list of paragraphs where each merely offers another example in support of the original, still inadequately vague, idea. For instance, consider this title: ' "Shakespeare's middle comedies explore the ambiguous boundary between playfulness and seriousness." Discuss.' A poor answer to this might be no more than a randomly ordered anthology of ambiguous moments none of which was used to reveal more than the student's agreement with the title's bald assertion. A paragraph would tend to begin by implicitly admitting the essay's failure to progress: 'One of the most notable examples in *Twelfth Night* where playfulness and seriousness mingle is the joke played against Malvolio by Sir Toby, Feste and Maria.' The structural weakness here betrays an intellectual floppiness back at the planning stage.

The writer should have thought about the precise implications of terms like 'playfulness' and 'seriousness'. There should have been curiosity about the various methods by which a literary and dramatic text can signal such a dichotomy of tone. There should have been discrimination between more or less evenly balanced attempts to both amuse and challenge an audience. One comedy should have been distinguished from another in terms of how, how often, and how insistently it offers such ambiguous moments. Had such issues been properly considered, the writer would have seen that a particular speech or scene needed to be considered at a specific stage of an overall, developing argument rather than just included anywhere.

A more promising start to a paragraph introducing the sub-plot's plot against Malvolio in *Twelfth Night* would be any of the following:

> The latent pun in 'playfulness' is far more relevant in *Twelfth Night* than in *As You Like It*. Malvolio is the victim of a play-within-a-play.

> Seriousness, however, is not just a matter of potential tragedy in plots which eventually still stagger to the relief of a comic conclusion. The voiced thoughts of the characters may be more or less serious as they try to make sense of the events in which they are involved. The ploy of inviting Malvolio to give portentous weight to a quickly scribbled forgery relies on his own gravity. The playful trick works because its victim takes himself so seriously.

> There are, however, episodes which impose more strain on an audience's capacity to laugh and sympathize at the same time. Is it the careless playwright or the carefully discredited character of Sir Toby who is the sub-plot's archplotter and goes too far in the joke against Malvolio?

Such poignancy may be only hinted in *As You Like It* but it recurs too often and too explicitly in *Twelfth Night* to be dismissed as incidental. Even the playful joke at Malvolio's expense soon becomes a serious exposure of human vulnerability.

ORDER OF COMPOSITION

You may some time be faced by an essay title which forces you to structure your entire answer according to the chronology in which a series of texts was composed. Far more often you will meet titles which merely seem to do so: 'Trace the development of Shakespeare's dramatic and poetic art from his earlier to his later tragedies.' Here there is no requirement to begin with a paragraph on the earliest play, and then simply to add discussions of other plays following the order in which they were written.

Indeed the title insists upon an alternative principle of division: the answer must distinguish between Shakespeare's 'dramatic' and 'poetic' techniques. You could even decide that every one of your paragraphs should itself commute between early and late plays to show advances (or, more neutrally, alterations) in the use of a specific device. You could design a thesis/antithesis structure around the question of whether it is specifically as a writer of verse or more generally as a playwright that Shakespeare changes most. In that case you would have to remember that the etymology of 'playwright' has nothing to do with writing but, like wheelwright or cartwright, records the craftsman's capacity to build parts into a whole which works well and looks good.

Some paragraphs of such an answer would concentrate on verbal texture. Others would examine the overall design which shapes the story and the more visual moments of the text where what characters can be seen to do is as significant as the speeches which allow us to hear their thoughts.

You could design a developing argument that the plays become less 'poetic' in one sense as in another they complicate their poetic artistry, making the manipulations of their verbal mannerisms less obtrusive and harder to resist. This might, or might not, lead you to open your essay with a series of plays in order of composition. More ideas might be conveyed by arranging the paragraphs into discussions of distinct topics like diction or metre or imagery.

You could then devote the second part of your essay to exploring 'dramatic'. You might seek to prove that Shakespeare's later plays define the possibilities and limitations of their theatrical medium quite differently from his earlier ones.

The danger of ordering your material around the order of composition is that it is so soothingly easy. It may distract you from the effort of deciding your own priorities. It may sap curiosity as to what is the most convincing sequence in which to explain your ideas. Where the question explicitly demands an interest in such chronology you must, of course, ensure that your essay constantly examines the relevance of that factor. Its significance, however, can seldom be lucidly debated in an essay whose own structure slavishly follows the order reported by literary historians. Their facts must be used to stimulate and support your own ideas.

THE TEXT'S OWN ORDER

A chronological structure, treating the parts of a long work in the same sequence that the reader meets them, has one obvious advantage. Loyalty to the text's own strategy may conveniently reveal what it actually feels like to be its reader. A text is itself an essentially chronological phenomenon. In its earlier passages it raises expectations in the reader's mind which may subsequently be fulfilled or frustrated. Later passages are decoded by the memory's recovery of previously planted signs. Where essay titles focus on a work's structure or story-line, your answer is likely at some stage to progress by following the text's own route.

But relying on that sequence for the ordering of an entire essay is rash. It risks paraphrase. An account of a narrative text may dwindle into mere plot-summary. The skeletal reconstruction of a polemical work may strip away the subtleties of its suasive rhetoric and the palpabilities of the factual evidence or emotive exemplars that it chooses to deploy. Commentary on a meditative poem may translate the flavour of its individual tone into the blandness of your own impersonal prose. Criticism is not story-telling. Nor is it translation from the text's own language. It is illumination of that language's precise means and effects. For instance, the importance of a particular device or implication may be that it recurs many times in a work. You may then need to gather into one paragraph examples which the text itself keeps apart.

Beginnings and endings

Someone may have told you that essay structure can rely on the simple formula of 'introduction, middle and conclusion'. In practice this leads some students to concoct a first paragraph which just announces their intention of writing an essay, and a last which merely claims that they have done so. The entire task of answering the set question and saying anything useful about the appropriate text is thus left to the intervening paragraphs. If these have been assembled according to no subtler principle than that enigmatic concept of a 'middle', they will be as shapeless and inert as a stranded jellyfish.

Forget 'introduction' and 'conclusion' until you have worked out a rational sequence for the main body of your essay. It is here that you will have the most interestingly difficult problems of discrimination and sequence. How do you keep each major topic or idea sufficiently distinct for the reader to know at any given moment just what is being examined or advanced? How do you, while keeping that present subject clear, ensure that the reader understands its dependence on what has been established earlier and its purpose in relation to what is yet to come?

If you solve these problems with sufficient care and cunning, you may find that you have designed a structure not just for the so-called 'main body' of your argument but for the entire essay: to add an introduction and conclusion would be superfluous.

Of course, there are legitimate uses to be made of introductory and concluding paragraphs. Faced by an unusually complex topic or an ambiguously phrased title, it may be necessary to devote a first paragraph to identifying problems and clarifying issues. So, too, there may be cases in which you feel it would be too frustrating to abandon your essay without a suggestive final paragraph to indicate how, if you had space and time to explore more texts or other controversies, your argument might develop.

Where such needs do not arise, and yet you still feel tempted towards that pair of extra paragraphs, ask yourself whether your problem is that they seem so easy to compose. What you could fluently express without the discomfort of any hard thought is almost certainly not worth saying.

Opening paragraphs seem particularly prone to platitudes and irrelevances, so it may be that you should force yourself to begin with a firmly stated idea which forms the first stage of your argument. You may, instead, be in the habit of offering information about a text's historical period, or the life of its author, or the view taken of it by some famous critic. The effectiveness of a factual opening will depend on your motives. It may be that you are merely trying to postpone facing up to the real challenge. You just feel nervous. Ideas seem risky. Facts, however irrelevant to the set question's specific demands or your eventual answer's chosen strategy, seem relatively safe. If you are merely doodling your way into an appropriately courageous state of mind, doodle on a separate sheet of paper, not in the first sentences of your essay.

You can test whether your introductory facts are just doodles by asking yourself these questions. Has the fact which I am about to offer been chosen carefully from a sufficient range of candidates? Do I understand how it is relevant to the title and why it is itself unusually thought provoking? Will my prose immediately explain what that relevance and those thoughts are?

Of course, texts do exist in contexts. Facts about the society that produced them or the ways in which they have been subsequently processed to colour the modern reader's approach may by crucial. Nevertheless, you cannot yet hope to be as well-informed on some areas as your teacher is. So a factual opening may have the inherent disadvantage of stating only what your reader already knows. If so, it will delay, however momentarily, your offering something which the reader does not find tediously familiar: the first of your own original thoughts.

Another popular ritual for limbering up before the essay

makes any pretence of performing its specific task, is a generalized claim to be thinking:

> The statement made in the above essay title certainly raises some important issues.

> In order to discuss whether this quotation is appropriate or not, it is necessary first to decide exactly what it means.

> There is no quick and easy answer to this question which can only be resolved after careful consideration of some specific passages.

Truly considerate critics keep such musings to themselves. At an early stage of preparation, they start thinking in more precise terms, defining exactly what the 'important issues' in this case are, and choosing the 'specific passages' which will be most illuminating. What they later share with the reader in an opening sentence is a stimulating idea about just one of these issues or passages. Their essays begin not by asserting thoughtfulness but by demonstrating it in the careful definition of a particular thought.

You can usefully aim for an opening idea that is so peculiarly apt to the set question's demands that, unlike the weak examples above, it could only be used to introduce the specified topic. But first sentences which just restate the title are useless. That is the one piece of information which your reader indisputably has in mind already, having just read it at the top of the page. Here is a question followed by the opening of a feeble answer:

> What is there in the poetry of the 1914–18 War besides decent human feelings of outrage and horror?

> To suggest that First World War poetry is merely used as a vehicle to express outrage about the long-drawn-out war and to depict with horror the anguish of the battlefield limits the works to being little more than protest poetry and anti-war propaganda.

Here the title's concepts are regurgitated rather than discussed. Some terms are simply repeated ('outrage', 'horror'). Others are translated by synonyms which may sound like variations but actually add no clarification or challenge

('1914–18 War' into 'First World War'). There is no attempt to probe the precise implications of the title's own chosen terms; to expose any hidden premises which these may contain; or to identify problems raised, but not explicitly stated, by the question itself.

Wasting even a portion of your opening statement on re-statement makes a poor first impression. If asked 'What is William Morris's view of the role of literature in political reform?', do not begin: 'In determining William Morris's view of the role of literature in political reform, it is imperative that we should remember'. Do not repeat the title's demands. Begin your response.

Perhaps the most popular of the exercises which may warm up the shivering writer, but eventually chill the reader, is a statement of intent. Here the first paragraph is devoted to summarizing what the rest of the essay will seek to prove. Thus views which may later be interestingly and convincingly argued are at first just asserted. Generalizations which later paragraphs could be going to test and qualify by analysis of specific evidence are first offered as glib banalities. Texts which the essay might eventually explore in detail and discriminate thoughtfully are merely listed; this reveals little more of the writer's ability than a knowledge of their titles.

First impressions must influence the reader's response in a critical essay as in any other text. Still, you may have fond memories of some novel even if you warn your friends that it makes a rather slow start. So make a special effort over your opening but do not fret about it disproportionately. Do try to find an immediately interesting point to make at the outset and do take extra trouble over its phrasing. Nevertheless, concentrate most of your efforts upon most of your answer. If that answer maintains a high enough quality of substance and form throughout, the lack of a dazzlingly perceptive opening will not much trouble your reader or diminish what you have taught yourself by writing the essay.

Endings, with a few obvious adaptations, should be constructed on the same principles as those which I have just outlined for beginnings. Merely winding yourself down and out of the tautest intellectual effort should be as private as the preliminary winding yourself up and into that properly productive mood. The general claim that you have been thinking, like the claim that you will be, can be no substitute for specific thoughts. Reminding the reader of the essay title should be even more superfluous by the end of your answer than it was at the beginning.

A merely summarizing conclusion is likely to be repetitive and reductive. Like any paraphrase, it is likely to do an injustice to the subtlety and complexity of the text which it seeks to abridge. You will often find that what you had planned as your penultimate paragraph should in fact be the last. If it establishes the final point of your argument, it will probably make a decisively detailed resolution which some more broadly-based summing up would only dissipate.

Admittedly, the position of your closing sentences gives them unfair advantage in any struggle to change your reader's mind. What has been most recently read tends to be most vividly remembered. So an undisciplined tutor may be excessively impressed by a final flourish or give a disproportionately low mark to an essay which falters right at the end into uncharacteristic clumsiness. Most tutors, on most occasions, however, can be relied on to read well. That means reading all of a work with equal attentiveness. Do end as clinchingly or wittily or thought provokingly as you can. Remember, however, that no localized spit and polish here will put a shine on an otherwise dull essay.

If in doubt, begin your essay no earlier than the beginning of your argument and, as soon as that argument is complete, stop writing.

4 Making a detailed case

Most O-level questions – and indeed many A-levels ones –
spell out the need to go into detail. You might now, however,
be faced by a question which sounds more generalized. Do not
be misled. Admittedly, as an advanced student, you should be
gradually learning how to offer more sophisticated thoughts
about a wider range of literature; but you will also be expected
to support those ideas by more skilful use of specific evidence.
Sometimes a title's phrasing will be deliberately vague in the
hope of provoking you into thinking and writing more exactly.
Choosing – and using – the most localized moments in a text
may now matter more than ever. So acquire the habit of
chanting to yourself, at every stage of essay composition,
'Specify; specify; specify'.

Clarification or proof

In literary criticism, as elsewhere, evidence can involve two
distinguishable concepts.

To make evident is to reveal. References to particular episodes, lines or words show your reader the text as you see it.
By citing examples you explain just what the patterns are that
you have spotted.

Evidence can also suggest the means of persuasion, the facts
and factors by which a case can be proved. You need not only
to explain what your contentions are but to demonstrate that
they are rational. Evidence proves that you are not guessing at
a distance but responding to words that all can find on the

printed page. What your own prose suggests must be shown to be at least tenable.

Should you go further? Should you organize the evidence into proving that your view is not just reasonable but right? Perhaps striving to change your tutor's mind is good exercise for your own.

There are various conventions which operate here and their relationship is problematical. Most tutors will want you to develop and express your own opinions but many will still deal harshly with an essay which sounds opinionated. An objective survey of available approaches is often welcomed as one ingredient of a student essay. Yet those students who devote the whole of their answer to reporting the views of others are likely to be condemned for failing to think for themselves.

You can present your case as if you were some honestly polemical barrister consistently arguing for one side in an imaginary court of cultural law. Many essays derive a useful clarity and vigour from trying to convince their readers that one conclusion is true and the alternative false.

You can, by contrast, attempt the objectivity supposedly achieved by a judge when summing up the conflicting evidence. Here all the relevant facts are recalled and discussed. Contrary views of their significance are explained as neutrally as possible. You can try to give some hypothesized jury of reasonable readers the materials on which to base their own decision.

Your own handling of evidence should probably adopt some compromise between candidly partial advocacy and meticulously impartial judiciousness. Any minimally competent barrister understands that simply to ignore the opposing evidence would be counter-productive. It must be acknowledged and weighed with perceptible fairness before being found wanting. Otherwise, the selectivity will be recognized as grossly misleading and the argument rejected. Conversely, the way in which a judge sums up rival bodies of evidence must in practice reveal some preference. The relative prominence given to particular facts, or to certain ways of interpreting them, will hint advice as to which verdict could seem slightly, but measurably, more appropriate.

Extremes are best avoided. Beware of devoting too much of

your essay's energy to persuasion as distinct from exposition. You need to reveal the text and to offer sufficient contradictory examples from it. Suppressing all evidence which embarrasses your present contention could blind you to the more fertile complexities and ambiguities which the texts contain. It may thus deprive your reader of what might have been your most interesting observations.

Excessive diffidence can be just as damaging. The neutral balancing act in which you sustain patterns of opposed but equally convincing evidence may seem graceful to you but could strike your reader as frustrating cowardice.

It may anyway be not just undesirable but simply impossible to disguise all your own beliefs about the deeper issues and murkier problems. Limits of space obviously prevent your reproducing every relevant text in its entirety. Yet such transcription would be the only strategy which could achieve strict accuracy. The episodes which your chosen allusions recall and the localized effects which your selected quotations emphasize will inevitably reveal some of your own priorities. Be conscious of this as you wonder what evidence to include. You can thus identify in time the sillier prejudices which must not be allowed, even through such discreet implication, to infiltrate your essay. Discriminate these from the more thoughtful principles which can be defended and which your essay should more frankly and systematically support.

Quotations

FREQUENCY

Literature tutors, when asked how often a student essay should quote, are likely to wriggle. They may retreat behind some version of that maddening, if honest, non-answer of 'It all depends'.

Some topics can hardly be treated at all without constant use of verbatim extracts. You might be asked to tackle 'How well does Keats rhyme?' Such an essay title amounts to a holdall containing numerous specific queries each of which can only be posed and resolved by quotation. For instance, stanza 7 of Keats's 'Ode to a Nightingale' meets the final tricky demand of its rhyme scheme through an inversion. The stanza does not fade away into 'forlorn fairy lands' but vanishes with more decisive poignancy 'in faery lands forlorn' (line 80). The next stanza begins in repetition as if to demonstrate the regularly echoing chimes within which rhyming texts must function:

> Forlorn! the very word is like a bell
> To toll me back from thee to my sole self!
> Adieu! the fancy cannot cheat so well
> As she is famed to do, deceiving elf.   (11. 71–4)

Does the use of 'elf' introduce connotations which advance the text's argument about the relationship between the factual and the fanciful? Does it instead sound like some desperately feeble attempt to make the best of a bad job imposed by the need of a rhyme for 'self'?

Yet that impotently twee image of the 'deceiving elf' could seem a fortunately unfortunate choice. It may sharpen, rather than blunt, the text's point. Those limits within which human aspirations must strive to express themselves do sound bitterly narrow. The bell-like rhyme forbids progress of thought and expansion of topic, confining the text's voice to discussing nothing but its own 'sole self'. The text enacts what it asserts, sounding as if the most imaginative hopes of escape from its self-regarding form do indeed prove deceptive. To comment upon the apparent purpose and actual effect of rhyme-words is clearly to quote them. So, too, most questions which depend on terms like 'style', 'language', 'diction', 'vocabulary', 'syntax', 'rhythm' or 'metre' will require almost unceasing use of verbatim examples.

Yet rules like 'Essays on structure and meaning need fewer quotations than essays on figures of speech' are unreliable. Story, sense and style are often so interdependent that critical debate about one has to encompass the others. Some questions may sound as if they are interested in the meaning of life. All answers must demonstrate curiosity about literature. You may anyway find, in studying your quotations (particularly those which tend to be cited often), that the meanings which we read into life have often originated in our literature.

Prose texts, like poems, are not plate-glass windows through which we gaze in order to see something else. You can approach them as toys or games inviting you to play with language. You may prefer to treat them more seriously as propaganda-machines whose linguistic components have been assembled to confirm or challenge your beliefs. In either case, novels are not natural phenomena but essentially verbal constructs, designed with varying degrees of skill, to entertain or manipulate.

You must quote if you are to reveal just how a novel's portrait of people and places and communities is contrived. Without examples to show the ways in which a prose fiction uses its language, your own prose can reproduce only a blurred image of what the text pictures in detail. You need to expose those verbal devices which shape and colour the reader's understanding of an event or a scene or a society. Even where your main aim is to interpret an openly didactic work, you cannot accurately identify its values unless you observe exactly how these are defined by the text's own terminology. Only verbatim extracts can show that what a work says depends on how it speaks.

If you are in doubt as to whether your essay is in danger of offering too few or too many quotations, err on the side of excess. Most tutors will be less resentful at having to read superfluous extracts from the text than at being required to decode your own prose where lack of examples has left it bafflingly obscure.

Moreover, copying out quotations, even if some are not strictly necessary to your argument, at least gives you the chance to notice more about their chosen terms and possible implications. So there may well be long-term intellectual gains to compensate for any slightly lower mark on this particular essay. By contrast, composing sentences which are culpably uninterested in a literary work's own choice of language will just reinforce the bad habits of your mind's laziest ramblings.

RELEVANCE AND LENGTH

An essay is an argument, not an anthology. There is no generosity in distributing quotations evenly throughout your essay as if you were sticking coins into a Christmas pudding. When you have nothing to say about a text, dotting extracts from it among your own vacuous remarks is no defence.

If you fear that you have still not thought up enough ideas, try to identify those passages in the text which appeal to you so much that you would like to be able to cite them. You may sometimes need to resort to this if you are to discover what you value in a work, and so stir yourself into conceiving an argument.

Once you have thus triggered some larger ideas, the process can thenceforward work in the more usual sequence: knowing what you mean to convey, you choose the most useful quotation to clarify and support each point.

A lengthy extract whose significance could be interpreted in numerous different ways may sometimes be essential. You could be arguing that a text's multiplicity of implication often depends on passages where ambiguities proliferate and the reader is compelled to think in many different directions at once. Nevertheless, there will be plenty of other moments where your essay is advancing just one, fairly simple, proposition. Then a short quotation which does not provoke too many other, distractingly irrelevant, ideas is best.

For instance, let us suppose that you have to discuss how far Tennyson's *In Memoriam* evokes the intimacies of family life. Perhaps you first want to establish a straightforward prima-facie case by showing that the poem often refers to marriage, parenthood and, more specifically, babies. Two out of the many available examples might spring to mind:

(a)
The baby new to earth and sky,
   What time his tender palm is prest
   Against the circle of the breast,
Has never thought that 'this is I:'

But as he grows he gathers much,
   And learns the use of 'I' and 'me',
   And finds 'I am not what I see,
And other than the things I touch.'

So rounds he to a separate mind
   From whence clear memory may begin,
   As through the frame that binds him in
His isolation grows defined.   (XLV, ll. 1–12)

(b)
>   but what am I?
> An infant crying in the night:
> An infant crying for the light:
> And with no language but a cry.   (LIV, ll. 16–20)

The first extract, (a), may raise more questions in the reader's mind than you can afford to answer at this stage. There are possible obscurities. You might need to explain, for instance, the fact of human physiology which is referred to in the third stanza's 'frame that binds': at birth the two halves of the skull are still relatively soft and mobile; only gradually do they harden and close together around the brain.

The extract's view of psychology could also confusingly delay your present argument. The poem suggests here that only through language do we acquire self-consciousness, and exile our newly defined selves into loneliness. Yet language is all that the text itself can offer. So this attempt to stand back from its own medium and somehow speak of all that we have lost through learning to speak is obviously problematical. The subtle ramifications here could be explained by citing many other paradoxical passages in which this poem seems to be its own most demanding critic. Yet, if you move on to such moments and investigate their implications, your reader will soon lose track of your original, simpler point.

The second extract, (b), with its reiterated insistence on infancy in a familiar form – the crying baby, afraid of the dark – seems far more convenient. It is also usefully shorter. All other things being equal, quotations should, like your own prose, function with maximal economy.

In fact, you may think that even (b) could be usefully pruned before being included in your essay. Perhaps later paragraphs are to provide sustained treatment of the poem's many, explicit references to language. If so, to quote 'no language but a cry' here could be confusing to a reader who needs to understand the divisions into which you are structuring your argument. Your present purpose is adequately served if (b) loses its last line. To include it might just make it harder for your reader to find, and focus on, those other words which do support the one proposition which you are now advancing.

How far you are justified in abbreviating a quotation depends on the point which it must clarify. If you had been asked to 'Discuss *In Memoriam*'s stanzaic form', you would be unwise to offer many quotations which, like (b) above, begin in the middle of a line. Only whole stanzas could support most of your points.

By contrast, a brief phrase, or even an individual word, can usefully be quoted in some contexts:

> In *The Heart of Darkness*, Conrad's choice of terminology often suggests that the agents of imperialism are not awesomely, but absurdly, sinister. The Manager is called a 'devil' but only a 'flabby devil'; the brick-maker is a 'papier-maché Mephistopheles'. Their 'backbiting and intriguing' is described simply as 'foolish'.

Here, to quote whole sentences would be ponderous and of little assistance to the reader in discovering what the essay means to suggest or why the writer believes it to be true.

Nevertheless, there are limits to how short a quotation can be made without becoming enfeebled. Here examples follow each other too rapidly to convince:

> In *Volpone*, Jonson ensures that the language of the theatre is constantly used by all the characters: 'plot', 'posture', 'epilogue', 'scene', 'mask' and 'action' are examples to be readily found.

This list would hardly persuade someone whose own memory suggested that the text did not in fact make 'constant' use of such terminology. The assertion that 'all the characters' employ it is dangerously extreme since 'all' is nearly always a strictly inaccurate word. Here, certainly, one suspects exaggeration. The most minor characters say so little that they are unlikely 'all' to include 'the language of the theatre' among their relatively few words. Moreover, the reader needs to be shown the context in which a term like 'plot' is used before being able to form a judgement as to whether this is 'the language of the theatre' or merely a reference to some conspiracy.

Since quotations should be positioned where they have a precise role to play in advancing your argument, the length of those that you do use must be appropriate. You need to give your reader as many words from the text as are strictly relevant to your present point: no more and no less.

ANALYSIS AND COMMENTARY

Choosing relevant quotations is not enough. You must explain their relevance.

Your introductory sentence must not be wasted on repetitive waffle ('Here is another highly interesting example of much the same technique') nor on imprecise praise ('The following lines seem to me intensely moving'). What the reader must know, before tackling each extract, is the precise point which it is meant to demonstrate.

Do not let your introduction and your quotation become a single, unpronounceably massive sentence. Only the briefest quotations can be understood if they are lodged as mere components within your own grammar. It is usually safest to end your own sentence with a colon before writing out the quotation and then to begin a new sentence after the quotation is completed.

Follow each quotation with some comment upon its detailed means and effects. Allow the reader to look first at the passage and reach his or her own conclusions as to whether it does broadly confirm your preceding assertion. Then draw attention to some feature whose significance may have been missed.

Extremely short quotations may, of course, be self-explanatory. If they have been lodged at precisely the right stage of your developing argument, the applicability of the few words that they contain will often need no further demonstration. Most of your quotations will, however, be long enough to admit of varying views as to which words matter most. Your own opinion on this should be clear. Invite the reader to notice some specific choice or arrangement of words. Explain why it interests you and how it clarifies the question at issue.

Few students make the mistake of hurrying straight on from a quotation without any comment whatsoever. Many do, however, tend to make a remark which is too brief and too vague. Consider this example from an essay on Shakespearian comedy:

> In *As You Like It*, Rosalind tells the arrogantly procrastinating Phoebe that she should be thankful for a good man's love:

Sell when you can, you are not for all markets.
Cry the man mercy, love him, take his offer.

> (III. v. 60–1, Arden edn, London, 1975)

This is eminently sensible advice.

The reader will want to know more about the detailed expression of these lines. What is it about the text's selection and ordering of terms here that makes the 'advice' sound so 'sensible'? Is it the commercial metaphor in the first line? Does that usefully drag the audience's mind back from the fantasy world of literary pastoral to the more familiar and practical one of the market-place? Or is the effect achieved more by syntax? Are the four, firmly imperative verbs ('Sell', 'Cry', 'love', 'take') almost bullying in their claim that they recommend no more than common sense must concede?

What too of the bluntly unqualified negative in which Phoebe is defined ('you are not')? Alternatively, could rhythm be the main manipulator here? Does the quickening pace of those three, short clauses in the second line, each beginning with a stressed monosyllable, suggest an almost exasperated tone of urgency? Essay-writers could quite legitimately hold various views as to how each of these factors should be weighted relative to the others. Indeed an entirely different set of specifics might be picked out as more relevant. What is essential is that some detailed analysis is offered to put intellectual flesh on emptily assertive bones.

Where the quotation is in prose, it is no less important to think carefully about how it defines its statement as well as about what it is saying. Consider this example of inadequate commentary on a passage from Johnson's novella, *Rasselas*:

Johnson shows that the Princess's dream of a pastoral life is just a fantasy:

> She hoped that the time would come when with a few virtuous and elegant companions, she should gather flowers planted by her own hand, fondle the lambs of her own ewe, and listen, without care, among brooks and breezes, to one of her maidens reading in the shade. (chapter 19)

> Obviously, she has not really thought what it would be like to live as a shepherd at all.

Here the final comment only repeats what was asserted when the quotation was being introduced. Any tutor who, even after reading the quoted passage, still cannot agree, or even understand, the student's interpretation, may resent the lack of any further advice.

The same quotation could have been followed by:

> The Princess's fantasy acknowledges no distinction between known present and hypothesized future. The ornamental gardening, which she already performs in her present role as a lady of leisure, merges into the sheep-farming which she cites as an example of her supposedly different existence in 'the time' which 'She hoped would come'. Repetitive syntax insists upon this confusion so that 'flowers planted by her own hand' sound suspiciously like 'lambs of her own ewe'. The possessive pronouns assume that the new life will admit as much egotism as the old. Other people will still be conveniently arranged about her as her 'companions'. They will still conveniently reinforce her own system of values and satisfy her desire for sophisticated entertainment since they will be 'virtuous and elegant'. Their industriousness or skills as workmates are not mentioned so the labour of an agricultural life is presumably unimagined. The animals will demand no more than the amusing or sensual gestures of affection with which she might already 'fondle' a cuddly toy. The farmland does not demand her presence in some field where work is most needed: the Princess can position herself according to comfort – 'in the shade'.
>
> The alliteration of 'brooks and breezes' sounds so suavely literary that we already hear her enjoying the future as a merely fictional text even before we are told explicitly that it does involve 'reading'.
>
> The formal control of such a long sentence anyway suggests carefully written rhetoric rather than spontaneously uttered speech. It thus prevents the Princess's vision of the pastoral from sounding like some neutral and impulsive response to natural landscape. It is just a 'virtuous and elegant' reconstruction of that refined world which she

already inhabits and which she recognizes through the texts that she reads.

So it seems perverse to complain that the prose of *Rasselas* is too inflexible for characters to sound distinct and developing. Where the characters claim most loudly that their minds are open to future possibilities, the text's obtrusively consistent style insists that it – and all the characters which it contains – must stay closed within its present structures.

This long commentary suggests the kind of observation which might be welcomed if you had been asked to write a critical analysis of just one chapter in the novel. In an essay on Johnson's overall achievement it would almost certainly be condemned as disproportionate.

You may often need to confine yourself to picking out just one or two specifics. Yet, however few features of a quotation you have time to mention, each must prove your willingness to notice details and to think about their precise significance.

Here is an example of what seems to me a reasonably proportionate amount of guidance on a quotation of average length from *The Vicar of Wakefield*, a novel by Oliver Goldsmith. The first sentence briefly establishes whereabouts in the plot the text chooses to lodge the passage which is to be quoted. The second gives broad warning of the extract's intent and tone:

> Having reached their destination, Primrose and his family once again go about setting up their ideal world of rustic virtue. Their bliss is reflected by the fecundity of the land and the beauty of their setting:
>
>> Our little habitation was situated at the foot of a sloping hill, sheltered with a beautiful underwood behind, and a prattling river before; on one side a meadow, on the other a green. My farm consisted of about twenty acres of excellent land.   (chapter 4)
>
> In this description, 'sheltered' is the operative word. Primrose's stronghold of domestic felicity is guarded by the ramparts of a natural world – wood, river, meadow and green. Yet the encroaching pressure of a more commercial value-system can be seen in that accountant's precision

about the number of acres and the use of 'excellent'. In the end, the land's excellence is not dependent on its being beautiful to look at and listen to (that charmingly 'prattling' stream clearly has nothing important to say); land is 'excellent' if it is productive and profitable to the owner who has invested his venture capital in it.

The commentary which follows the quotation here centres on just two terms – 'sheltered' and 'excellent'. Yet an interesting argument about the text's values is initiated and convincingly shown to derive from close reading of the novel's own prose. The number of details noted in discussing a quotation is often, as here, less important than the precision with which they are used.

A less thoughtful student, having quoted the same passage, might easily pick out many more words to quote again in the commentary and yet say far less:

Many of Goldsmith's terms here are tellingly apt. Most of the adjectives, for instance, are particularly felicitous choices – 'sheltered', 'beautiful', 'excellent'. The characters are shown to be well-pleased with their new home. The nouns tell us more than enough about the scene to explain why they find it so attractive. We are given a clear picture of the 'habitation' beneath the 'hill', the 'underwood' in the background, the 'stream' in front, the 'meadow' and 'green' on either side. How carefully the novel here informs us about its setting, even to the point of calculating the farm's size as 'about twenty acres'. We are guided to hear as well as see the 'river' since 'prattling' is such a brilliant adjective to describe it.

The first commentary surely reveals more exactly what the passage may be suggesting. It wastes less space on what all readers are bound to notice and concentrates on more debatable implications which can explain the student's own response and judgement.

Sometimes, however, quantity – though still a secondary consideration – is important. If you ask your reader to work through an unusually long quotation, your subsequent commentary must be expansive enough to justify the exercise. Students who quote an entire paragraph running to ten sentences but then fail to say anything about nine of them will be suspected of wasting time.

Nurture your commentary so that it grows out of what you have discovered the quotation to actually contain and imply. Do not impose a view based on no more than an assumption about what the extract is likely to offer.

Here is an example of a student merely guessing from a broad knowledge of the text what the relationship between two quotations is likely to be. The essay is about Shakespeare's *Measure for Measure*, a text which elsewhere does indeed draw a strong contrast between the two situations to which the quotations refer:

> Claudio and Juliet's liaison is described positively. It is a truthful, fruitful, enduring relationship based on genuine love. Lucio remarks:
>
> > Your brother and his lover have embrac'd;
> > As those that feed grow full, as blossoming time
> > That from the seedness the bare fallow brings
> > To teeming foison, even so her plenteous womb
> > Expresseth his full tilth and husbandry.
> >   (I. iv. 40–4, Arden edn, London, 1965)
>
> This illustrates the delight in the beloved. Intercourse is not just a bodily function but an expression of binding love. By contrast, the libidinous Angelo gloats:
>
> >   I have begun,
> > And now I give my sensual race the rein:
> > Fit thy consent to my sharp appetite . . .
> > By yielding up thy body to my will.
> >   (II. iv. 158ff., ibid.)
>
> The language here is entirely different. Angelo reveals his violent, destructive surrender to overwhelming lust. He feels compelled to violate Isobel, to enjoy a bestially savage triumph over her.

In fact, however surprising to those who remember the overall pattern of *Measure for Measure*, the ways in which these particular passages describe human relationships may not be so tidily opposed.

Had the student looked in detail at the language of each

quotation, interesting complications might have been exposed. The first extract may be about an affair which the audience knows to be 'not just a bodily function', but these lines are not the source of that knowledge. Lucio's vocabulary does indeed include 'love', but not as an abstract ideal. Here it is a concrete noun identifying Claudio's mistress. Similarly terms like 'embraced' and 'womb' can be used metaphorically, but here Lucio's statement insists upon their literal application. His point is that the couple must have 'embraced' in a thoroughly physical sense because Juliet is now pregnant.

The chosen terms for this fact all have agricultural, as well as sexual, connotations. Thus 'teeming' can mean not only child-bearing but also crop-producing; 'tilth' can suggest any kind of productive labour (such as Claudio's virile effort) or more specifically the farmer's tilling which makes soil produce a rich harvest. In this context, the first two syllables of 'husband[-]ry' do evoke heterosexual role-playing but the complete word still carries its customary association of looking after farm animals. Juliet then is cast in an implicitly earthy role. Her fertility is that of the efficiently ploughed field and Claudio's attitude to it here sounds close to that of a cattle-breeder labouring to expand his herd.

Conversely, the second quotation credits the lecherously undisciplined villain with an unpredictable degree of self-control. Elsewhere the plot admittedly does suggest that Angelo is the helpless slave of his own dictatorial lust. Here, however, desire sounds less innately 'overwhelming' than the student claims. The equestrian image may confess that the speaker's sexual instinct is no more sensitive than a horse's; yet the masterful rider is evidently Angelo himself. It is he who decides when to let his libido have free rein and, by implication, how far it should be allowed to gallop before once again being restrained.

Too many students make this curious mistake of failing to read their own quotations. Here is another example taken from an essay on Marlowe's *Tamburlaine*. The writer begins with an assertion about the hero's enemies but then unhelpfully chooses to quote a speech by Tamburlaine's best friend:

> Tamburlaine is described by his enemies as a squalid thief and yet one whom they must fear. Techelles, his most admiring follower, describes him dressed for war:

As princely lions when they rouse themselves
Stretching their paws and threatening herds of beasts,
So in his armour looketh Tamburlaine.

(I. I. ii. 52–4)

The imagery used when describing Tamburlaine consists of constant comparison to Heaven, the Sun, gold, jewels, tempest and the Universe.

This final list surely needs more thought. How far is the play's respect for the cosmic ('Heaven' and 'the Sun') at odds with its commercial values ('gold, jewels')? Moreover 'the Universe' so nearly suggests everything that it means almost nothing. The major frustration, however, is that the one image quoted – that of regal yet savage animals – fits none of the categories to which, the student claims, 'constant' reference is made. Such chasms between an essay's argument and the passages which it chooses to quote are disaster areas which your reader must be spared.

You must also, of course, read again thoughtfully – and offer observant comments upon – any extract you include from a work of criticism. Whenever you quote a published opinion, comment clearly to show whether you agree or disagree. Be precise about just how far your support or scepticism goes. Offer your own (not the critic's) choice of evidence from the text itself to explain why you think the published view is right or wrong.

Your evaluation of each published view should be not only clear but succinct. Consider these pairs of alternative versions:

Smith's excellent book on these poems – and I agree with it absolutely here – suggests that:

Smith shrewdly remarks that:

I think it is useful to quote here the views of Jones, who, contrary to all that I have just shown, claims that:

Jones perversely claims that:

In their notes to an edition of this work, Smith and Jones offer the following comment which certainly seems relevant at this point:

Smith and Jones comment:

Preliminaries can thus be neatly brief.

The guidance offered after your reader has considered the quotation will nearly always need more space. If the remark is worth citing, its detailed implications deserve explanation. If it directly helps your own argument to advance – even when it does so only by exemplifying the weakness of some alternative approach – its exact contribution needs to be defined. Where you discover that these conditions do not apply, delete what must be an unwarranted interruption of your own prose.

Paraphrase and plagiarism

When you want to refer to someone else's published opinion, do try to use a verbatim extract. Where you cannot find a sufficiently succinct quotation with which the critic's view can be characterized fairly, you will have to paraphrase. Beware. The risk is that you will fail to make it absolutely clear that this material is borrowed even though its abbreviated expression is your own. So, before you begin to summarize any idea from a published essay, name its author. Begin with some version of 'X writes that' or 'Y's approach is to'.

Do not start off by offering the idea, intending later to add some retrospective statement such as 'this point is made by X'. At best, such a sequence temporarily misleads. Your reader begins to remember having read the same series of observations elsewhere and cannot yet be sure that the debt will be properly acknowledged. At worst, you could forget to admit the loan and to identify the lender. Then you will never be able to prove that you were only being absent-minded, not deceitful. Legally, the unacknowledged use of an author's ideas or words is an offence. The laws of copyright make published material the author's personal property. Brief use of it may be made provided the precise source is explicitly acknowledged. Surreptitious use of it, deliberately misrepresenting the borrowed as the invented, is plagiarism which the law treats as theft.

Of course, you may believe that ideas and their verbal formulations should belong equally to all and that here at least, in intellectual capitalism, property can itself be theft. You may anyway think that a far more widespread common ownership already exists. Perhaps you accept the existence of a massive, if predominantly hidden, web which binds your thought to all the texts that you have read and connects them to many others. If so, acknowledging those few, relatively minute, threads of influence which your memory can consciously retrace may seem an oddly limited project.

Nevertheless, in other contexts, knowingly to present someone else's work as one's own does strike most people as obviously unfair. In the academic world, nearly all teachers disapprove of unacknowledged borrowing and a few go almost hysterical when they discover it.

For a student, plagiarism is so counter-productive as to be not just squalid but simply illogical. It cannot assist you in any of the purposes which have led to your writing the essay. It actively discourages the exercise of those intellectual muscles by which you hope to develop the strength and flexibility of your own mind. It is itself so dishonest that, far from increasing your or your reader's chances of approaching nearer to the truth, it must reduce them.

Most students, of course, quite reasonably, also want to impress their tutor and gain a good mark. But even these objects are likely to be defeated by unacknowledged borrowing. Consider how much better-read most tutors are than most students. Remember, too, how similar are the skills required by the tutor as literary critic and the tutor as thief-catcher. Expertise in analysis of style and evaluation of argument tunes the ear into those subtle inconsistencies of phrasing or thought which mark the joins in scissors-and-paste fraud. The likelihood of plagiarism being found out is extremely high. Its punishment is almost certain to be severe. No gambler who could add up would accept such a risk for such paltry gains.

If you are interested enough in improving your own criticism to have read this far, you are obviously not going to waste your time in cheating. However, plagiarism is still your problem. Others do cheat and your tutor will not, at first, know you well enough to have blind faith in your good sense and honesty. Your essay therefore must provide detailed reassurance throughout. Since you are a borrower at risk of being mistaken for a thief, explain clearly who has lent you what idea and just how much use you are making of it.

Your first essays may thus have to confess to being far more derivative than you would wish. Fear not. More image-enhancing originality can be claimed later when you are able to offer it. Meanwhile, you must concentrate on persuading your tutor to become your ally. His, or her, support is, and will be, needed. In the short term, your tutor may be your most crucial adviser as you work to turn yourself into a better critic. In the longer term, your paths may cross again. There may be examinations to take. You may want a job reference. Whatever naïvety or ignorance you must at first confess, your tutor should still be willing to provide all the help you want both now and in the future. If, however, you have once allowed your reader to mistake you for a crook, you had better look elsewhere for assistance. Your tutor will be busy with more certainly deserving students.

Specifying without verbatim extracts

At certain points of your argument, you may be able to make sufficiently precise reference to the text without offering quotations. It may be no less illuminating – and demonstrably far quicker – to write of 'the scene where A first meets B' than to copy out a massive chunk of their earliest dialogue. It may be more sensible to describe a passage of a long poem than to quote it. At certain moments in a discussion of *Paradise Lost*, you might write of 'Satan's soliloquy on first reaching Eden' rather than guess how many of its 182 lines your reader will be prepared to plough through for no better reason than to discover what passage you are talking about.

Numbers may sometimes be adequate: 'In the last scene of Act III' or 'only ten paragraphs after the beginning of the novel' or 'throughout stanzas 6 and 7'. Vaguely describing some feature as 'often' present in a poem will be unconvincing. Yet you need not quote every passage in which it occurs. You might write simply that it occurs 'in no less than seven of the twenty-six lines which comprise the entire work (lines 1, 4, 8, 9, 14, 20 and 21)'.

Sometimes even substantial issues can be economically raised by arithmetic although the discussion will soon need to proceed to quotation:

Though a superficial digest of the plot might suggest that *Dr Faustus* constructs an evenly balanced debate between the virtuous and the vicious, the Good Angel is allowed only twenty-four lines. The speeches of the arch-tempter, Mephistophilis, on the other hand, are exceeded in frequency and length only by those of Faustus himself. However, not all of Mephistophilis' lines serve the diabolic cause. Consider, for instance:

[quotation]

Naming names can also succinctly specify examples to prevent an assertion seeming hopelessly vague. Do not write of 'some characters' but of 'some characters, such as —— and ——'. If you are making a claim about what 'many of the poems' do, at least offer the titles of two or three which demonstrate what you have in mind. Do not leave your reader wondering whom you might mean by calling some attitude 'typical of eighteenth-century essayists'. Name some. So too, expressions like 'it has often been argued that' should immediately be supported by naming one or two of the published critics whom you are remembering.

Names, like numbers, or any other factual specifics, must be constantly subject to the 'So what?' test. They only help if they fuel the drive of your argument. Information is not necessarily evidence. Its relevance to the literary problem which you are investigating must be shown. Consider this: 'Alexander Pope was born in 1688 to Roman Catholic parents. He was well-educated but had to be privately tutored since, as a Roman Catholic, he was banned from the universities.' Here 'Alexander' is unnecessary for identification: there are no other considerable poets of the surname. The forename should either have been excluded or used to begin discussion of the works:

> Pope's parents chose to call him Alexander, reminding us that the poet's mature delight in the epic gestures of ancient history is no personal idiosyncrasy. It is an almost inevitable response to the intellectual habits of his society. Pope's translating *The Odyssey* and colouring so much of his original verse with echoes of ancient models (*The Aeneid*'s underworld transformed into 'The Rape of the Lock''s Cave of Spleen, for instance) are symptomatic of the climate into

which he was born. He is exploiting the points of cultural reference by which his generation of English intellectuals has been trained to order their understanding of the contemporary scene.

Similarly, the precise date of Pope's birth 'in 1688' might have been cut as wholly irrelevant to his works. Would any poem have had to alter its stance or style in anticipation of a significantly different audience if its author had been born a few years earlier or later?

Alternatively, the date should have been used:

> Pope was born in 1688: that pivotal year in British history which seems oddly apt to the poet's later, ambivalent stance. The verse is at once deviant in its protests against, and conformist in its compliments to, the values of the English establishment. In 1688, seven bishops of the Church of England were tried for daring to criticize James II's policy of toleration towards Catholics. Yet 1688 later ushered in 'The Glorious Revolution' when the fleeing James was replaced by the confident Protestantism of William III. Pope, the religiously deviant Roman Catholic and yet politically conservative monarchist, creates verse which commutes uneasily between the almost blasphemous subversiveness of 'Eloise to Abelard' and the virtually propagandist reverence of 'Windsor Forest'.

Neither of these expansions has yet arrived at a quotation from any of Pope's poems. Yet each uses specifics (such as titles, for instance) to turn biographical fragments into the beginnings of a critical argument.

5 <u>Style</u>

Remember the reader

Never forget that what you are now writing will have to make sense to someone else. If that reader is – however indirectly – your examiner, you will score points not for what you had in mind but only for what your prose manages to say. Inefficient prose simply fails to communicate. Unless your style speaks clearly, no other virtues or skills which you may possess can be recognized.

Of course all readers need to be motivated. Tutors, too, want to be interested. They may even hope to be amused. So try also to inject some vigour into your style. You can raise your reader's hopes with a first sentence which is phrased arrestingly. You can leave behind a good impression with a last sentence which is phrased memorably. The more of the intervening sentences which seem well-written and even witty the better. Alertness to any ambiguities and playfulness which may lurk in the language of your own prose should anyway help you to notice and enjoy more of the verbal games that literary texts are themselves playing.

But an over-ambitiously original style may stumble into pretentiousness or wander away into mere eccentricity. Posturing and whimsicality infuriate some tutors, and all resent word-play where it is irrelevant. Ensure that any imaginative expression is indeed designed to express rather than merely impress. If it defines your meaning more precisely or conveys it more economically, use it. If not, settle for a simpler, more direct, phrasing. Some tutors may welcome verbal wit as a bonus. What all insist upon is a style which shows them how much you know and what you think.

Clarity

USE FAMILIAR WORDS

Good criticism of literature does not itself strain to sound literary. If you try to use unfamiliar words merely to sound sophisticated, you will just distract yourself from the task of making your meaning clear. Such pretentiousness may even tempt you to use words whose precise meaning you do not know. Then you risk writing gibberish.

Of course, you should aim for a gradually broadening vocabulary: the wider the range of terms from which you can choose, the more likely you are to find those that will define your point with maximal economy, clarity and precision. Moreover, a relatively complex language may be necessary even to think certain ideas. Nevertheless, longer, less familiar words chosen just for their length or obtrusive learnedness will merely slow pace and muffle thought. Compare these alternative versions of the same point:

> The play commences by making manifest the ruminations of its hero.

> The play starts by telling us what its hero thinks.

The latter is far more likely to help writer and reader into a real curiosity about whether the claim is accurate and relevant.

Here are two more examples of pompous circumlocution, each followed by a more direct paraphrase:

> Shakespeare desires in the first scene of A Winter's Tale to demonstrate that Leontes is perusing his wife's social gestures towards their guest with close attention and some alarm at the possibility of sexual impropriety.

> Shakespeare means in the first scene of A Winter's Tale to show that Leontes is anxiously watching his wife's behaviour towards their guest. Already he suspects an affair.

James Joyce was not ignorant of the fact that human beings are not always *au fait* with what passes in their own minds and not always able to organize their observations into a logical sequence.

Joyce knew that thoughts are often unconscious and disorderly.

You may find that simpler phrasing exposes in time how simple a proposition you were about to offer:

In *Henry IV*, Hal becomes subjected to a process of education which finally enables him to assume with full competence the duties which pertain to monarchy.

In *Henry IV*, Hal is gradually taught how to be a good king.

Such a point, however straightforward, may still seem important enough to be included in your essay. However, you must eliminate the verbal elaboration before you can decide whether the idea is sensibly unpretentious or damagingly naïve.

USE MODERN ENGLISH

Criticism is addressed to readers now. It is not aimed at the first readers of an eighteenth-century poem or even at the original audience of an Edwardian play. You should use modern English unless quotation marks make clear that you are offering a verbatim extract from some text written at an earlier stage of the language's development.

So good literature should be 'praised' not 'lauded'. Ill-tempered characters should be credited with 'anger' not 'ire'. Fast-moving prose may still have 'speed' but no longer 'celerity', and, even at its most efficient, should not now be described as 'efficacious'. Satirists no longer 'mercilessly vilify' those whom they 'abhor' even if they still 'repeatedly attack' those whom they 'dislike'.

In your own prose, find modern equivalents for the text's archaisms and more remotely literary terms. You will then sound properly curious as to what these do in fact mean.

You must, however, balance the advantages of a modern

style against the need to evoke a text's own, perhaps out-moded, texture. The main mechanism for maintaining this balance is quotation: your own contemporary English intro-duces the reader to verbatim examples of the text's earlier usages. However, in some cases where it is not appropriate to use quotation marks you may still need to reproduce loyally the text's own archaic terms. It is no use referring to what a Restoration comedy calls a 'serving-woman' as an 'au pair' or a 'daily'. Texts often use a different vocabulary because they reflect a different society.

USE SHORT SENTENCES AND STRAIGHTFORWARD SYNTAX

Write shorter sentences wherever you can. A sentence which you cannot pronounce aloud without pausing for breath is almost certainly too long. Split it in two (or three). Doing so will force you to think more precisely about the various points which your unwieldy construction had tried to combine. Dis-criminate between these ideas. Work out exactly how they are related. Then express them in a rational sequence of far briefer sentences. Your prose will be at less risk of sounding clumsy or pompous. More importantly, it will make immediate sense.

Sometimes, of course, you may discover that a lung-burstingly protracted sentence has not grown as a result of having so many ideas to express. Instead, it is making only one point, but at inordinate length. Then prune accordingly.

Sentences have various purposes. However, each sentence can only be asked to perform one main task if it is to do it well. Ask yourself what each of your sentences means to achieve. If it seems to have more than one function, be suspicious. Consider dividing it into shorter statements.

Here are three of the many tasks that a sentence might be performing. It could be an assertion about how a text (or some part of a text) should be interpreted. It could be a description of what kind of literature or literary device can be recognized in a text. It could be a judgement on how successful a text is. A single sentence can hardly ever contain interpretative, descriptive and evaluative thoughts without muddling them:

Hamlet is essentially about the hero's struggle for sanity in a world of baffling contradictions but, being a typical tragic drama of its period, it tries to enlist the audience's support for an act of revenge and the play is thus often distracted from its subtle characterization of the Prince's thought-processes by a clumsy pursuit of melodramatic plot.

By forcing three distinguishable ideas into a single, blurred statement, the writer fails to explain how they relate. An alternative version might be designed in three sentences:

Hamlet may often seem to be about the hero's struggle for sanity in a world of baffling contradictions. However, at moments it is still typical of its period in encouraging the audience to support a decisive act of revenge. So the play is often distracted from its subtle characterization of the Prince's thought-processes by a clumsy pursuit of melo-dramatic plot.

Clearer though this draft is, it may still ask each sentence to do too much. In the last sentence, for instance, there are two judgements – one positive ('subtle') and one negative ('clumsy'). Perhaps each deserves a sentence to itself.

Moreover, the division into more sentences reveals how many large, ill-defined and unsupported claims are being made here. Perhaps each needs to be followed by extra sentences which offer further definition and supply some specific evidence to show how tenable the idea is. Shorter sentences will not just make your argument clearer to the reader. They may reveal to you in time that the point you were about to make is too bald to be convincing.

You will often have to compose a sentence whose job is to define more precisely the claims made in the previous one. For instance, the suggestion that the play is 'about the hero's struggle for sanity' might be expanded by the following sentences:

Hamlet strives to make sense of contradictions which could drive him mad. There is Claudius, an honoured king who has committed a squalid murder. Almost as baffling is Ophelia, a prudish young girl who is willing to prostitute herself as a spy. The hero wrestles with such paradoxes in bewildering isolation, resorting to soliloquy because he is deprived of dialogue. His one surviving parent is in love with his father's murderer and the friends of his student-days are now his enemies.

Design a prose-style which pauses frequently to begin a fresh sentence. It will encourage you to move on from a generalized premise and advance to specific points.

Beware of compressing both an idea and the evidence which supports it into a single sentence. The result is usually inelegant and obscure:

> It is not so much Hamlet's dark clothing and bitter remarks in the opening scenes as some of his almost reckless behaviour in later scenes (his wild gestures towards Ophelia, his rash killing of Polonius) which make us wonder about his sanity (although, of course, it is possible to interpret his apparent madness as feigned for purposes of political prudence until the very end of the play).

The student should have spotted when drafting this sentence that it attempts to use too many different moments in the play. Unless your point is to compare or contrast, a sentence which is about more than one passage is likely to be over-ambitious. Divide it.

Another warning sign in the example above is the use of brackets. Do not interrupt or extend a statement with some parenthetical addition which deserves a sentence in its own right.

The ratio of one sentence to one idea is a guideline not a rule. There are contexts in which each of your sentences may need to encompass a pair of points. Then there may be a risk of monotony and you must consider another guideline: sentences should vary in structure and in length.

In answering 'Compare and contrast' essay titles, your prose may get stuck in a recurring structure. You may repeatedly deploy some formula such as 'On the one hand in X . . . but, on the other hand in Y', or 'Whereas in X we find A, in Y we find B'. A sequence of sentences where each begins 'Whereas' can be tedious to read. Try to vary your syntax.

The content of the following sentences is meant to offer helpful advice. Their structure, however, should demonstrate the difficulties of reading prose whose grammar is repetitive:

Whereas the dull sentence tends to be long, the interesting sentence is often short. Whereas the dull sentence tends to vagueness and repetitiveness of terminology, the interesting sentence usually deploys precise words each of which is used only once. Whereas the dull sentence tends to offer generalizations which might apply to almost any text, the interesting sentence frequently offers close observation and verbatim quotation. Whereas the dull pattern of unvarying syntax tends to drive one barmy, imaginative variation in the ways that each sentence begins, proceeds and ends may keep a reader awake.

Arousing interest is, however, a secondary consideration. Your first must be the clear and precise communication of your thoughts. If your prose is flexible enough to keep matching its style to its substance, your sentence length and syntax will vary.

USE OF THE PRESENT TENSE

The rule requires '*Beowulf* achieves [not 'achieved'] more than most Anglo-Saxon poems'. 'Romeo loves Juliet' is acceptable; 'Antony loved Cleopatra' is not. You should write 'Jane Austen here means [not 'meant'] to be funny'. These are not arbitrary conventions. They are rational practices on which criticism's commitment to precise accuracy depends.

The text which your essay is discussing cannot be recalled as a past event. To do so would imply that it has become a permanently closed book. In fact, the very existence of your own essay proves that the text can still be constantly reopened, reread and reinterpreted. It is a resource whose present availability is indisputable.

Each reader of a story, even a reader who has read the whole of that story before, begins the first line in imagined doubt as to what the last will reveal. Whenever you are describing some particular episode within a narrative, you should report its events in the present tense. Only this can reflect the tension then present in the mind of the imaginatively curious reader.

There are, of course, remarks about books which do require the past tense: 'I first tried to read *Robinson Crusoe* when I was still at primary school and did not understand a word of it.' This statement could be a wholly proper one to make in conversation; but you should not write it in your essay. There you must concentrate on what you still understand and value in *Robinson Crusoe* – however long it may have been since you last read it. The present tense of critical prose helps you to focus on those ways in which a text is still alive, still able to stimulate and modify thought. Such surviving powers – as far as they are discoverable and describable – do belong in your essay. Points where the text is now dead to you should stay buried.

The characters in plays, novels, short stories and narrative poems are similarly only worth discussing because they come to life in minds now. Of course, some of these modern minds may be sufficiently informed and sophisticated to use fictional characters as a means of structuring images of past cultures. Modern readers may use the characters of an Elizabethan play or of a Victorian novel to understand the attitudes of some long-dead generation, and criticism is properly interested in how the first audience of *Julius Caesar*, or the first readers to buy a copy of *Oliver Twist*, are likely to have responded. However, your main task in considering characterization is to define the precise way in which a printed text available today still compels its fictive personages to act, and the exact signals by which it still manipulates the reader into a particular view of human nature.

The convention of the present tense discourages sentimental confusion between artificially constructed, literary personages and actual people who once lived as autonomous individuals but are now dead. Fictional characters spring to new life each time a fresh reader opens the text. They are ready to perform the same actions within the same verbal pattern in any passage which a reader may care to find. They are creations, still being produced by the text's choice and arrangement of language. They are thus at once more enduringly dynamic and more repetitively static than human beings. We must eventually die; but until then we can change. They always live to fight another day for some new audience or readership; yet they are confined still within the same lines of recurring signals.

Some modern critical theorists might argue that this exaggerates the difference. Perhaps the supposedly independent and unpredictable lives which we ourselves lead are also preordained by linguistic structures even if these are far more various than those which restrict literary characters. Our vaunted individuality may not be a liberty which we seize but a licence which words grant. Perhaps only through words do we become sufficiently discriminating to identify ourselves and sufficiently audible to be recognized by others. Without personal pronouns and personal names, could we tell ourselves apart?

Some critics would now argue that it is the English language that speaks us rather than we who deign to speak it. You may have no individual intellectual existence beyond the innumerable texts which have ordered your thoughts. You will not yourself have directly read most of these texts. Yet their vocabulary and usage may have influenced the phrasing of some speech that you have heard, or contributed to the style of some book that you did once read. They may thus have indirectly determined how you will decode the next of those relatively few works which you will read for yourself.

Perhaps there is a never-ending interdependence through which understanding of one text is programmed by knowledge drawn – however unconsciously – from others. Such intertextuality may mean that even a work which is now scarcely ever read is still influencing the language in which we shape our ideas. These views – just as much as traditionalist ones – suggest that describing any work in the past tense as if it is a spent force must be misleading.

For not unrelated reasons, authors as interesting, historical personalities who once led idiosyncratic lives seem unimportant to many modern critics. You may still believe that the purpose which a work was designed to serve is discoverable; you may consequently wish to write in terms of its author's apparent intentions. If you do leave the secure grounds of the text to enter the danger zone of literary biography, tread warily. Return as soon as possible to observing only those authorial choices which can still be seen at work in the text. These must be reported in the present tense. Those ideas or actions of an author which are not recorded within the work under discussion may tempt you to use the past tense, but they are likely to be irrelevant. By contrast, where you do instinctively feel that the present tense is appropriate, you are probably responding to what the text's own voice still presents.

Try anyway to reduce the frequency with which you refer to an author and to increase your references to a text: wherever you are about to use a writer's name as the grammatical subject of a sentence, consider substituting the title of a relevant work.

Economy

BE BRIEF

Some tutors specify a minimum number of pages which the essay must reach. Such demands must be met by finding enough to say: not by saying little at excessive length. At every stage use only as many words as are needed to advance your argument, or to make it more comprehensible, or to render it more convincing. Any word which does none of these wastes both your own and your reader's time. It also makes it harder for you both to notice the words that do matter. After composing one verbose paragraph you may be unable to spot, among the mist of superfluous verbiage, the relatively few points which it has made. If so, you will begin the next paragraph with a hazy sense of direction. You may lurch off at a tangent; or repeat a stage of the argument which has already been sufficiently explained.

Your reader, too, wearied by struggling through redundant or repetitive phrases, may be tempted into skip-reading. There is no guarantee that the skipping mind will consistently leap over the meaningless froth, and keep landing on the meaningful stepping-stones. It may do precisely the opposite. Then your essay will not just be criticized for taking too long to say what you think. It will be condemned as failing to demonstrate any thought at all.

DO NOT PROMISE: PERFORM

Essays often waste words in laboured statements of intent:

Before embarking upon a detailed analysis of the actual text of Conrad's *Lord Jim*, it might not be inappropriate to look at some remarks about the project made by the author himself in letters to his friends at the time he was writing the novel.

Perhaps the reader will soon be interested to read the extracts from Conrad's letters, and will later be impressed by 'a detailed analysis of the . . . text'; but no points can be gained here by the assurance that these will eventually be offered.

You can see for yourself why most of the words in the sentence are mere padding. However, one clause exemplifies a surprisingly common redundancy: 'it might not be inappropriate to'. Other popular versions of this formula are: 'It is interesting to examine', 'It is worthy of note that', 'It is significant that', 'We must not forget that'. Any point you are about to make obviously seems to you appropriate and interesting. You would not deliberately exasperate your reader. If the ensuing material is irrelevant or dull or trivial, no preliminary appeal can persuade your reader to see it differently. If it is well chosen and well phrased, its effect can only be weakened by any delay in reaching it.

Explicit claims of accuracy are often delaying mechanisms too: 'We can say with some assurance that', 'It is indisputably apparent that', 'The way that this scene should be viewed is'. Less shamelessly bullying but just as useless are the following: 'So we see that', 'We may therefore conclude that', 'Thus it can be seen that'. These last three tend to be so ubiquitous in students' essays that you can soothe your reader's nerves simply by cutting out every use of them before handing your own work in. Of course the conjunctions ('so', 'therefore', 'thus') will often need to be retained if the skeletal form of your developing argument is to stay clear. Just prune the flabbier verbiage which they so often trigger.

Promises of a judicious balance in your approach, or of a willingness to support it with closely observed evidence, are similarly no substitute for performance. Spot the redundancies here: 'Yet, to be fair, there are some passages of *Don Juan* where Byron is not so evasively humorous but instead offers a more committedly serious tone. On closer examination it can be observed that'. All critics, one piously hopes, mean 'to be fair'. Any explicit claim that you, too, prefer not to cheat just wastes space and arouses suspicion. The insistence, at the beginning of the next sentence, that the text will be closely and observantly examined also protests too much. The reader may fear that an essay so proud of doing its job here may not bother to do so elsewhere.

THE IDEAS IN YOUR ESSAY ARE ASSUMED TO BE YOUR OWN

Do not begin a sentence with 'I think' or 'I feel' or 'I am not unaware' or 'I hold the view that' or 'It is my own opinion that'. Use your first words for a thought. Do not waste them in announcing that, when you do get around to offering a thought, it will be your own. Your reader is not likely to mistake it for the word of God, or a report by the Arts Council, or some involuntary burp from the collective unconscious.

Similarly, there is no point in writing 'I would argue that' or 'I would maintain that' if you are about to do so. Nor is it helpful to preface your ideas with 'I believe that' or 'I am persuaded that' – unless you have the reputation of a liar. Other wasteful announcements that you are still alive and well and living somewhere in your essay's argument are: 'in my view', 'in my opinion', 'for me', 'as I see it' and 'it occurs to me'. So long as you are arguing and offering evidence – rather than merely making undefended assertions – you will sound sufficiently modest. Laboured use of the first-person singular pronoun can in fact make your essay sound self-centred where it should be centring on the text.

Using 'one' or 'we' instead of 'I' might seem less egotistical. Yet these can sound presumptious in some contexts and evasive in others. They should certainly not be deployed with 'I' to concoct chaos:

> One could argue that the individual lyrics of *In Memoriam* are components in a unified artistic whole especially if we, as I do, take Tennyson's overall theme to be, not grief at the loss of a friend, but panic at the loss of religious faith.

There are two escape routes from this dizzying oscillation between self-assertion and passing the buck. The essay could have specified some published critic who advances the view, and then, offering reasons for scepticism, dissociated itself. Alternatively, the approach should have been phrased as implicitly the student's own:

The individual lyrics of *In Memoriam* are not isolated fragments evoking grief at the loss of a friend. They are components of a unified artistic whole whose theme is panic at the loss of religious faith.

Wherever you feel tempted to use 'one', ask whether it represents your own view or that of someone else who deserves specific acknowledgement. When you are about to write 'we', ask who else's agreement you are assuming and how well founded that assumption is. Are you lazily taking your reader's support for granted rather than going to the trouble to argue your case?

At the very least, spare your reader either of these clichés: 'One may therefore conclude that', 'Thus we see that'. Conclusions drawn, and views held, by your essay are known to be your own. If they are feeble, the reader will not be persuaded that the blame lies with some third-party 'one' and will resent being included in a conspiratorial 'we'. If what you 'conclude' or 'see' turns out to be interesting, you should not interpose such empty gestures but allow your reader to reach it immediately.

AVOID REPETITION

Perhaps the commonest source of uneconomic writing is a compulsion to say the same thing twice. Repetition rears its ugly heads in such Hydra-like profusion that I can only identify one or two of the most popular formulas below. You must therefore defend yourself by asking, throughout the writing of your essay: have I said this before?

Nervous writers prefer to dress each concept in at least two words as if one on its own might fail to prevent indecent exposure. This belt-and-braces strategy praises the 'emotion and feeling' of some texts while condemning others as 'shocking and horrifying'. It describes virginal characters as 'pure and unspotted' or 'blameless and innocent'. It describes tougher types as incapable of 'love and affection'. They may even be 'ruthless and unrelenting' in their 'cruelty and viciousness'.

In this idiom, satirists treat unjustifiable 'pride and self-esteem' to 'ridicule and mockery'; or rebuke it, in a 'grave and serious' tone of 'didacticism and moralizing'. They have to protest 'strongly and forcefully' since 'collapsing standards and moral sickness' are 'increasing and expanding'. Indeed the 'adequacy and effectiveness' of 'values and principles' are being 'challenged and questioned'. At the more 'crucial and significant' moments of literary history, saying everything twice may not be enough: after all, 'the Romantics who favoured imagination and fantasy' were, according to one student's essay, outgunned by a three-pronged attack from 'Augustans who prized knowledge, information and facts'.

The emptiness of such treble-talk, and even of the more common doublings, may look relaxingly obvious when so many examples are removed from their original contexts and juxtaposed. Be warned. Pairs of virtual synonyms can infiltrate even the most vigilant first draft. When revising it, look specifically for every phrase in which 'and' yokes two nouns, adjectives, verbs or adverbs. When you find one, ask yourself: what is the difference between the connotations of these two terms? Has that distinction been explained? Or could both words be suspected of saying the same thing? Of course, if they do turn out to offer almost identical meanings, you must retain the more apt or vigorous term and cut the other. Here is an extract from an essay on Shakespeare's *Richard II*:

> Unlike Richard who is so hysterical and excessive, Boling-broke has the strength and ability to remove those who endanger the state.

This could be expanded to distinguish the paired terms:

> Richard's despairing speeches in Act III sound hysterical just as his complacent demonstration of authority in Act I looks excessive. The less flamboyant Bolingbroke, by contrast, has the intellectual strength to identify those who would endanger the state and enough ability as a military strategist to defeat them.

The alternative is simply to prune the original down to:

Unlike the hysterical Richard, Bolingbroke does have the
ability to remove those who endanger the state.

In trying to eliminate this particular kind of redundancy from
your essays, you may have to resist the blandishments of
alliteration. Surrender to them will not make you sound 'cunning and calculating', though they too often cause 'fear and
foreboding', or even 'torture and torment' in students' essays
and tutors' minds. Alliterative redundancies like 'pathos and
poignancy' will not meet a 'sensitive and sympathetic' response. Two words which share the same initial letter may
sound to you as if they belong together. They do not, if the
context allows them to mean much the same.

To avoid another frequent source of repetition, do check
your longer sentences to ensure that all are making progress
and none is circling back to its starting-point. Beware the kind
of sentence which begins 'Hardy is a pessimist' and concludes
that 'his novels do not sound hopeful'. Even if intervening
clauses between the two halves of such a repetition are full of
interesting movement, the surrounding stasis will still bore.

Whatever kind of inattention has led you into a repetition,
do at least avoid any laboured confession. To tell the
reader that your next words will add nothing new is hardly
diplomatic and yet versions of the following are frequently
sprinkled through students' essays: 'We have already seen
that', 'As explained before', 'As I have said earlier', 'It seems
worth repeating here that'. To a demanding reader nothing
will seem 'worth repeating'. The admission that you know
your structure has led you into redundancy but that you cannot
be bothered to revise it may seem rudely inconsiderate. Ideally
eliminate all repetition. If some does remain, at least be
discreet and then, however undeservedly, you may escape
censure.

Precision

Precision in literary criticism is both a commitment to strict
truthfulness and the means by which that is achieved: close
observation. You must, of course, observe precisely what
words the text itself chooses and exactly how it deploys them.
Only then can you form a sufficiently accurate view of how it

works. To express that view clearly and fully, however, you will need to be just as precise in selecting and arranging your own terminology.

GENERALIZATIONS TEND TO BE FALSE AND BORING

A course in literature may eventually help you to develop clearer opinions on large issues. You can quite legitimately see it as a way to arrive at your own definition of literature and your own theory of its function in forming minds, shaping cultures and controlling societies. However, if broad ideas are to have any impact, they must demonstrably derive from close attention to fine detail. Had Darwin failed to offer precise observation of specific examples, his theory of how species evolve would probably be incomprehensible. It would certainly be unconvincing. You, too, must patiently examine the apparently trivial and fragmented. Only then will your judgements on larger relationships be worth reading.

Inclusive, unqualified statements tend to suppress relevant distinctions and implicitly to deny exceptions which may matter. So the more broadly you generalize, the less likely you are to be accurate.

Even where a generalization is sufficiently guarded to be true, it may be such a self-evident truism as to be useless: 'The importance of love to Shakespeare varies enormously from play to play but all his works are to some extent interested in human relationship.'

A precise observation on some specific aspect of one particular play would clearly seem fresher. The amount of localized effects assembled within one text is so vast that your own choice as to which words deserve comment is unlikely to duplicate any other reader's selection. Conversely, the more general the point which you offer, the more likely it is to be an idea which your reader has met many times before.

Be wary of using too many plural nouns. These tend to proliferate where precision is being abandoned in favour of generalizations too sweeping to be useful: 'Fools and rogues are to be found throughout Shakespeare's plays.' 'In Dickens's heroines we witness the emotional and moral qualities he most admires.' Any statement about all the works of an author is at risk of being a banal truism or an untruth. So, too, are remarks about the ways in which all their characters or events are presented: 'D. H. Lawrence's novels involve contrast (and even collision) between the realistic and symbolic levels in which events are presented. Visual descriptions and allegorical patterns of imagery conflict.'

Superficially this last example may impress as more sophisticated than the first two. Yet each of the plural key-phrases in its second sentence is in urgent need of support from a singular observation: an example to prove that Lawrence's attempt to make a scene visible does, at least once, get in the way of its symbolic function.

Criticism often needs to identify what is singularly interesting about a particular work or passage. What is singular is seldom best defined by a flood of plurals.

Be sparing too with abstract nouns. The more inclusive the noun the less usefully precise it is likely to prove. 'Life', to take an extreme example, can hardly ever deserve a place in your critical vocabulary: 'This work sometimes aspires to be an enquiry into the very nature of life itself.' Does this say anything? Life, in at least some of its myriad forms, is presumably evoked by any text from a train ticket to a television programme guide. Nothing earlier in the quoted sentence limits the almost limitless range of connotations that 'Life' might suggest.

The following sentence, from an essay on T. S. Eliot, may sound less obviously naïve but does it say anything more? '"The Wasteland" is given artistic depth by its philosophical profundity.' The nouns 'depth' and 'profundity' are being used metaphorically here, in an abstract rather than a concrete sense; so your suspicions should be aroused. Grammatically, both may be qualified by adjectives, but 'artistic' and 'philosophical' are themselves epithets of such unqualified vagueness here that they can hardly qualify the latently multiplying implications of the nouns.

Perhaps the most regrettably common abstract nouns in literary criticism are that dreary pair 'appearance and reality'. Too many fascinatingly distinct texts tend to be reduced with mechanical consistency to 'studies/exposures/explorations' of the 'contrast/conflict/dichotomy/gulf/gap' between 'appearance and reality'.

The problem is greater than just that of a cliché which is too hopelessly wide in its applicability. Students, in writing of 'appearance and reality', tend to blind themselves to the intrinsic oddity of literature itself. Literature, by definition, uses the strange arbitrariness of black marks on a white page to manipulate our definitions of what is true. The inky appearances, reaching us through printer, publisher, distributor and bookseller somehow determine what our culture accepts as reality. Even works of so-called fiction redesign our view of fact.

If you banish the phrase 'appearance and reality' from your critical vocabulary, the search for substitute terminology will usually lead you to make some less generalized, more usefully precise point.

DANGEROUS TERMS WHICH NEARLY ALWAYS NEED FURTHER DEFINITION

'Realism' is as problematic a concept as 'reality'. In most contexts you can simply avoid calling a work 'realistic' or 'unrealistic'. Where you must use the term, accompany it immediately by an explanation, preferably citing specific examples, to show just what level of credulity the text seeks and what methods it uses in trying to achieve it. Milton's gigantic, winged angels and Jane Austen's demurely clean-thinking heroines may strike you as equally distant from people you know. Even so, the ways in which *Paradise Lost* and *Emma* admit their own artificiality are quite distinct. Trying to find synonyms for 'realistic' will help you to be – and therefore sound – thoughtful. At the very least it will alert you to the fact that 'realistic' is sometimes used to mean 'pragmatic', 'unsentimental' or even 'cynical' instead of 'life-like' or 'credible' or 'naturalistic'.

'Naturalistic' has an uneasy relationship with 'natural', which in itself can be a confusing word. It will often be one of those importantly mobile terms which the work under discussion is itself seeking to redefine. Nature – like so many key-concepts – tends to be what texts make it. Consider the fact that in Europe at the beginning of the eighteenth century poets write as if it is natural to look away from a mountain peak as a grotesque deformity marring the elegant face of the created earth. By the end of that century the literary convention was to assume with equal certainty that anyone who fails to respond to the grandeur of the Alps or the Lake District is behaving so 'unnaturally' as to be hardly 'human'.

Writers often use the word 'natural' to describe qualities which they regard as peculiar to people. Yet calling behaviour 'natural' may also invoke qualities which we have in common with those other species who must survive in the same world as we do – the survival instinct itself for instance. Consider the elusive mobility of the term's implications in the following extracts from students' essays:

> Samuel Johnson's 'The vanity of human wishes' suggests that not only greed and ambition but also piety and pity are natural.

> Donne's verse centres on natural emotions and 'The Exstacy' argues that copulation, even for the most intellectual men and women, is still a necessity.

> It was quite natural for Jane Austen as a privileged woman of the time to be uninterested in either the Napoleonic Wars abroad or social unrest at home.

> T. S. Eliot in 'The Four Quartets' favours the natural existence of medieval peasants over the artificial life led by twentieth-century London's lower middle classes.

> In spite of his being a professional soldier, Macbeth's killing of his King is so unnatural that the whole order of Nature is disrupted.

> Shakespeare shows that Lear's unnatural egotism drives him mad and the hero's insanity then deranges his entire society.

The last example suggests another set of terms which must be used guardedly: 'madness', 'sanity', 'rational', 'deranged' and similar words. If an 'entire society' behaves in a certain way can that behaviour seem 'deranged'? Does 'madness' by definition mean little more than what the prevailing standards of a particular society regard as extremely abnormal behaviour?

What a seventeenth-century love-poet thought reasonable as a definition of a human relationship might strike an eighteenth-century essayist as insane in its perversely impassioned hyperbole. Moreover intelligently deviant texts may challenge even those definitions of acceptably rational behaviour which their own contemporary societies favour. A list of authors who have been diagnosed as dotty by contemporary reviewers might constitute, in the mind of a radical critic, a roll of honour.

Madness is arguably one of those redefined topics whose growing prominence in writings of the late eighteenth and early nineteenth centuries constitutes a phenomenon called Romanticism. This involves another set of terms that you must use with care. Much Romantic poetry is explicitly opposed to those values which 'romantic' in ordinary modern usage evokes. Shelley's 'Epipsychidion', for instance, describes the convention of monogamous marriage in terms which Barbara Cartland's readers could hardly approve:

> I never was attached to that great sect
> Whose doctrine is that each one should select
> Out of the crowd a mistress or a friend
> And all the rest, though fair and wise, commend
> To cold oblivion, though it is in the code
> Of modern morals, and the beaten road
> Which those poor slaves with weary footsteps tread,
> Who travel to their home among the dead
> By the broad highway of the world, and so
> With one chained friend, perhaps a jealous foe,
> The dreariest and the longest journey go.   (ll. 150–60)

When E. M. Forster quoted from these lines in the title of *The Longest Journey*, he was announcing a novel whose view of human relationships could be described as 'soberly *un*romantic'. Yet the lines do adopt a convention-defying stance which some literary historians would call characteristically Romantic. Get such discriminations clear and be sure which kind of romanticism you wish to suggest before using the term. When you do use it, design a context which will allow your reader to know precisely what you mean.

Even if you determinedly use 'Romantic' in the literary, as opposed to popular, sense, there are still distinctions to be drawn. Do you wish to make a reference to English or, more broadly, to European Romanticism? If the former, do you use the term merely to identify a chronological period and apply it to any work at all that was written between, say, 1780 and 1830? Or do you mean the adjective to be descriptive, crediting some text with certain characteristics which you think typify a particular kind of literature that was produced at that time? If the latter, you must make clear exactly what characteristics you have in mind.

The same care must be used with comparable terms like 'Augustan' or 'Victorian'. If you call Webster a 'Jacobean' dramatist, do you mean no more than that he was writing during the reign of James I rather than a few years earlier when Elizabeth I was on the English throne? Or do you hope to suggest particular changes in theatrical and literary fashion? If so, be precise about what qualities in Webster's work do strike you as significantly typical of the later period's dramatic literature.

'Dramatic' is itself another word that in a literary context carries specific connotations quite different from those which a non-specialist might intend. The writer of a critical essay should remember that 'dramatic' has definite associations with a particular medium or genre. Do not use it as a casual synonym for 'exciting', 'eventful' or 'strikingly emotive'. If a poem or novel reminds you of theatrical conventions you need to show your reader just where and how and with what effect it does so.

I have been able to discuss here only a few of the many terms that critics need to use with care. You might make your own list of other words that will usually need to be supported by localized definitions before the reader can know what is intended. When you want to deploy such a term, ask yourself what it can mean in the context of the particular text under discussion, and make sure that your answer is included in your essay.

ELIMINATE PHRASES WHICH IMPLICITLY CONFESS VAGUENESS

Spot the admissions of woolly-mindedness in the following: 'This speech's fragmented syntax, boisterous rhythm and so on suggest a comedy of sorts. A good many of the words have a kind of wild energy, an almost obsessed type of joy and excitement.' The frustrated readers, of course, are left to find their own answers to the essay-writer's begged questions. Which unmentioned specifics could have been added at the point which the phrase 'and so on' leaves vague? What particular 'sort' of comedy? Just how 'many' of the words have what exact 'kind of' energy?

That evasive phrase 'type of' raises particular problems with its confusing implication of the typical. Consider: 'Marlowe's Faustus is a representative of a certain type of Renaissance intellectual.' This presumably is a long-winded attempt to call Faustus 'a typical Renaissance intellectual' but to do so would not, of course, be sufficient. Would you understand what was meant if you were described as a 'typical twentieth-century intellectual'?

If the student had worked towards a sufficient knowledge of Renaissance thought, the essay could have offered a more helpfully precise version: 'Marlowe's Faustus typifies the sceptical, almost cynical, energies of those Renaissance intellectuals who were closer to Hobbes than Hooker.' It may, however, be safer to avoid mentioning 'types' at all since there is the inherent risk of reductively stereotyped thinking in using the term: too many texts and too many of their individual components can lose their shape when critical prose squashes them back into some larger, more amorphous mass – the blancmange that supposedly typified 'Augustan literary convention' or 'Victorian uncertainties' or '1930s *Angst*'.

Here is another example. It offers at least four overt warnings that the writer is not choosing to be precise:

> In *As You Like It*, Corin and Touchstone are somewhat akin
> to the traditional double-act with a 'straight' man or what
> you might call a fool. It is here that we are reminded that the
> differentiation between 'proper' theatre and what we
> would probably describe as Vaudeville or Music Hall did
> not exist in Shakespeare's time. Yet there is something of a
> failure in the play's 'jokeyness'.

'Somewhat akin' does not tell us how close the writer judges the comparison to be. The quotation marks round certain words signal enough intelligence to suspect their appropriateness or propriety but not sufficient industriousness to seek out more certainly accurate substitutes. Whether the reader 'might call' the character 'a fool' is no business of the essay. Its task is to commit itself to its own decisions as to the truest terminology. There is similar evasiveness in 'what we would probably describe as'.

The 'something of a' formula is used by cowards who dare not write what they mean ('there is a failure'); or by fools who do not know what they mean: 'something' could be anything and so defines nothing.

'Some', 'sometimes' and 'somehow' should also trigger alarm bells when you are checking a rough draft. Are you adding sufficient detail to answer the begged questions?

FIND PRECISELY APT TERMS OF PRAISE OR BLAME

Terms which merely assert admiration can sound like damningly faint praise. Too many writers, when describing a work which they think not just good but unusually good, call it 'great'. They thus evade tricky questions about exactly what kind of interest it arouses and precisely what skills it shows in doing so. Other words like 'powerful', 'effective', 'significant' and 'important' also tend to dodge definition of the particular means used to achieve specific effects.

The following extracts offer other adjectives which shout a hurrah but hardly say anything:

> Goldsmith's handling of the couplet form in 'The Deserted Village' is magnificent.

> Throughout *The Faerie Queene* Spenser uses beautiful imagery.

> The seventeenth chapter of *Oliver Twist* is one of the most meaningful in the novel.

This last makes me wonder whether the writer thinks the worst chapters are quite meaningless. The need, clearly, is not to assert the quantity of meaning but to move straight to the task of defining its precise quality.

A surprising number of students use 'poetic', 'unpoetic' and even 'poetry' as evaluative terms. Byron's arguably sentimental love-lyrics are admired as being 'very poetic' but his more urbanely cynical jokes in *Don Juan* are condemned for being 'unpoetic' or 'merely verse rather than poetry'. This is wrong. 'Poetry' defines a kind of writing in contradistinction to prose. If the author – not the printer – chose where each line should end and each new one should begin, the text is not prose but 'poetry' or its synonym 'verse'. Even if a work of verse is almost unreadably incompetent, it remains to the critic a poem.

Whatever word you are about to use in praising or attacking a work of literature, ask yourself at least two questions. Firstly, does this word merely say I like/admire/am impressed by (or alternatively I dislike/do not admire/remain unimpressed by) this? If it only announces pleasure or pain, consider discarding it. Secondly, wonder how many other passages of this and other texts could be truthfully described by the same adjective. If you need to count on the fingers of both hands, try again to find a term more precisely apt.

Of course, jaded terms can be brought to life. 'Brilliant' actually sounds woefully lacklustre in most contexts but does function here: 'Milton's celebration of God's light in *Paradise Lost* is literally brilliant, revivifying the old symbolism of divine radiance with images as precisely visual as those that make Satan's "darkness visible".' 'Impressive', too, can be redeemed by immediate answers to the questions of what impresses the reader and how; or by exploiting the latent pun (physical pressure and, more specifically, printing).

Do not, however, be tempted to make weak adjectives sound less empty by filling them out with supposedly strengthening adverbs. Claiming that you regard a text as 'absolutely fascinating' or 'extremely significant' or 'remarkably poetic' or 'truly magnificent' will not disguise your failure to identify exactly what qualities you admire and why.

Incidentally, consider abandoning the use of 'very' even in front of the most carefully chosen adjectives. You will probably find that omitting it makes your criticism in fact sound more convinced and convincing.

DO NOT MAKE EXAGGERATED CLAIMS FOR YOUR OPINIONS

You cannot bully the reader into believing that your view is the only sensible one. The following formulas and all their dogmatic variants are likely to be inaccurate and unconvincing: 'It cannot be denied that', 'No one can ignore', 'All readers must feel that', 'It is impossible to doubt that'. Some readers are remarkably stupid and may well be able to miss a point which to you seems obviously important. They may not deserve your consideration but your own reputation for thoughtful truthfulness does. Other readers, in spite of being highly intelligent, might just dare to diverge slightly from even your favourite opinion. They do merit your respect and one of them may be going to read your essay.

Consider this: 'The reader cannot help but be amused when Oscar Wilde remarks in "The critic as artist" that "there is no sin except stupidity".' Surely a thoughtful guess at the responses available to Wilde's readers here might hypothesize a less helplessly single-minded consensus. Some readers, at whatever risk of sounding pompous, might wish to retort that the intellectual snobbery celebrated in the epigram can be as offensive as the simple-mindedness it decries; or that one strenuously achieved belief, however clumsily expressed, could seem refreshing to anyone who has endured too many of Wilde's casually assembled denials of value; or that reading prose composed of richly witty aphorisms is like ploughing through a whole box of chocolates. Such readers can 'help but be amused' and the effort may help to keep their critical eyes open.

The formulas which deny exaggeration itself are even more obviously useless: 'It would not be extravagant to claim that', 'It is no exaggeration to say that', 'It is impossible to overstate the case for'. You cannot bully the reader into using your own yardstick. Such claims are superfluous where the statements which they introduce sound reasonable. Where they may not, your sense of proportion, though loudly trumpeted, will not change your reader's.

SOME WORDS NEARLY ALWAYS LEAD TO OVERSTATEMENT

Hardly anything worth critical comment appears at all points in all of an author's works. Sweeping generalizations sweep relevant exceptions under a carpet beneath which your most impressively observant reading will be invisible. So beware

terms like 'all' and 'always' and their equally unhelpful opposites, 'none' and 'never'.

A critical essay is only enfeebled by the hyperboles which
can often invigorate comic poems. Consider Dryden's demolition of Shadwell, one of his many rivals in Augustan verse:
'The rest to some faint meaning make pretence/But Shadwell
never deviates into sense' ('Mac Flecknoe', ll. 19–20). The
unqualified decisiveness of 'never' succeeds in being funny. It
also assures us that the judgement is not offered seriously. The
laws of chance will allow even the most idiotic writer oc-
casionally to make some kind of sense, however worthless
Shadwell's random collisions with meaning may have been.

An overstated case is unlikely to be believed. Claims that
'Tennyson's verse is always lyrical' or that 'all Browning's
poems focus on character' or that 'none of Pope's lines sound
clumsy' or even that 'Dryden himself never deviates into
nonsense' will suggest ignorance of the texts or a casual
disregard for what your own words must strictly mean.

Even a Shakespeare play cannot be 'unfailingly' subtle
'everywhere'. Even a novel as ramblingly open-ended as
Joyce's *Ulysses* is not about 'everything'. Even a poem as
serious as *Paradise Lost* cannot be truly said to provide 'nothing'
for the reader's sense of humour. You might draw up your
own list of words which, in nearly every context, will prove
false. You could begin by adding to those mentioned above the
following adverbs: 'totally', 'wholly', 'completely', 'utterly',
'perfectly' and 'faultlessly'. The alert, critical mind tends to
have reservations. It notices exceptions. Write accordingly.

OVERSTATEMENT AND UNDERSTATEMENT IS A MATTER OF
DEGREE AND CONTEXT

Criticism may sometimes need to sound confidently incisive if
it is to cut through to the roots of an issue. An endlessly
tentative beating about the bush may circle around all sides of
the debate without itself advancing a contribution:

> In attempting to assess the achievement of Samuel Johnson,
> it would perhaps be insufficient to concentrate on a single
> work since some of his concerns are arguably recurrent,
> however varied in treatment. So it might be more appropri-

ate to wonder whether *Rasselas* and 'The vanity of human
wishes' can be seen as companion pieces even if contrasts
between the prose of one and the poetry of the other may
strike some readers as equally relevant.

This does not sound judiciously hesitant. It suggests a lazy
evasiveness which refuses to confront the relevant questions.
A more promising version might be:

Rasselas and 'The vanity of human wishes' do share some
qualities. They are unashamedly oratorical in style. Their
structures are episodic. Both works flatter the reader by
providing characters who can be comfortably patronized.
Yet even at precisely comparable moments clear distinctions can be drawn. Each text closes its sequence of
metaphors with the image of a powerful river and of people
being carried along by its current. Yet in the novel it evokes a
serene passivity whereas in the poem it defines an appalling
helplessness.

Johnson's own criticism can seldom be accused of timidity.
Here is one of his sturdier remarks: 'Why, Sir, if you were to
read Richardson for the story, your impatience would be so
much fretted that you would hang yourself' (Boswell's *Life of
Johnson*, 6 April 1772). You might enjoy the uninhibited theatri-
cality of this attack or resent its tactics as insultingly simple.
Perhaps there is as much imaginative vigour and more intellectual substance in Goldsmith's complaint: 'There is no arguing
with Johnson, for when his pistol misses fire, he knocks you
down with the butt end of it' (Boswell's *Life of Johnson*, 26
October 1769). Or is this as unhelpfully rough in its browbeat-
ing as the gesture which it attacks?
    Both assertions have an aggressive punchiness which is fun.
Yet, since neither offers supporting evidence, they seem unlikely to influence the reader's own view of either Richardson
or Johnson. Such attacks will sound disproportionate or apt
according to the opinion which the reader has previously
formed of the target texts. If you already believe Richardson's
plots to be relentlessly dull, you may welcome the ruthlessness
of Johnson's unqualified comment. If not, you will dismiss it as
a self-indulgent overstatement. If you also think that such
irrational dogmatism typifies Johnson's criticism, Goldsmith's

protest will sound shrewd rather than shrill. His metaphor of the failed duellist resorting to blunt thuggery will illuminatingly encapsulate your own suspicions.

Convincing criticism often reflects the tone of the work's own verbal texture. A short essay about a long work needs to be particularly wary of sounding too hasty in its judgements. Here is an example from an essay on a complex, ruminative novel about the interaction between distinct social, religious and racial groups:

> In *A Passage to India*, E. M. Forster deals with the offence which is caused by associating individuals with stereotypes. Adela Quested, brought up in England as a Christian, asks the Indian, Doctor Aziz (who believes in Islam), how many wives he has. In this case Aziz should not have felt insulted. His fault is being too sensitive and too ready to put a wrong interpretation on comments offered innocently by someone who means no harm.

The terminology here – 'offence', 'should not', 'wrong', 'innocently', 'means no harm' – sounds too decisively moralistic. The reader may feel distanced from the text's own tentatively balanced exploration of mixed motive and multiple responsibility.

Obviously an essay must be more economical in style than the longer texts which it describes. However, your brevity need not create a more dogmatic tone than the text has itself chosen. Here is a more appropriately cautious treatment of the same novel:

> Forster may explore the damage caused by people who pigeon-hole each other as stereotypes. Adela's curiosity about polygamists does make Aziz fear that she is less interested in him. Yet, even here, Forster's wide-ranging sympathy will not allocate simplistic blame. Adela may be being unimaginative and Aziz hypersensitive but both are victims of forces as impersonally vast as the subcontinent itself.

This last sentence perhaps offers such a grandiose assertion that it should immediately be followed by a quotation from the novel. Loyalty to the text's tone cannot long be sustained without a verbatim example.

AVOID SEXIST TERMINOLOGY

Literature is written and read by women as well as men. Your prose, if it is to be accurate, must reflect this simple truth. Do not use the masculine pronouns ('he', 'him', 'his') to denote either the typical author or the typical reader. Ezra Pound spoilt a thoughtful remark with one thoughtless pronoun: 'You can spot the bad critic when he starts by discussing the poet and not the poem' (*A.B.C. of Reading*, London, 1951, p. 84). This exclusion of women from the ranks of bad critics is not some outmoded gallantry. It smuggles in an ignorant insult by suggesting that women are not worth considering as critics at all. However, substituting 'he or she' may introduce a clumsiness. One solution is to pluralize: 'You can spot bad critics when they start by discussing the poet and not the poem.' Alternatively, an abstract noun can embrace both genders: 'You can spot bad criticism when it starts by discussing the poet and not the poem.' So do not write of 'the reader' and 'his response'. Write of 'readers' and 'their' response or of 'the readership' and 'its response'.

In many cases the problem can be side-stepped by rearranging syntax or by simply identifying and removing a redundant phrase without which there is no need of a possessive pronoun: 'The bad critic starts by discussing the poet and not the poem.' Prune terms of gender wherever gender is meaningless or irrelevant and you will often gain a bonus in finding ways of making a sentence sound more graceful and less wordy.

Student essays sometimes deploy 'lady' as a patronizingly polite evasion of 'woman'. If you are going to refer to male characters in fiction as 'men', you should call female ones 'women'. 'Lady', like 'gentleman', is only useful where you wish to stress a character's advantages of wealth, power or social status in the hierarchy of a class-conscious text. So do not be tempted to write of a 'lady novelist', a phrase which may acknowledge the charming amateur only to deny the impressive professional.

Some feminists would argue that 'mankind' as a collective noun for women as well as men sounds unbalanced. Certainly the blunter term of 'Man' can seem startlingly inappropriate: '*Gulliver's Travels* also offers a hideously detailed description of the skin on a female giant's breasts. This passage is perhaps the work's most telling magnification of Man to expose all that makes him ugly.'

Here is a more seriously confused and confusing extract from an essay on Webster's *The Duchess of Malfi*:

> The heroine is the one character who consistently shows the most admirably human and humane characteristics. In spite of all that her sadistic brothers and their henchmen have done to those she loves and to herself, she tells the jeering man whom they have sent to strangle her 'I am Duchess of Malfi still'. In this proudly defiant line she claims and proves that Man, even at the moment of his own death, can and should respect himself.

The heroine here could be said to assert the dignity of 'people', of 'humanity', of '*Homo sapiens*', even of 'men and women', though 'women and men' might seem fairer. However, if those 'sadistic brothers' are any guide to a masculine ethic, she hardly typifies 'Man'.

Consider, too, the vexed issue of authors' names. The convention which your tutor may still expect you to follow discriminates female authors by using forename as well as surname throughout: 'Woolf' is preceded by 'Virginia', and 'Plath' by 'Sylvia'. Male writers too may be given a forename or initials at the beginning of an essay but are thenceforward more economically described by their surnames only. 'E. M. Forster' after his first appearance thus becomes plain 'Forster' and 'Ted Hughes' becomes just 'Hughes'. So an essay on George Eliot reminds us throughout that the pseudonym masks a woman and she will still be, laboriously perhaps, called 'George Eliot' even in the essay's last sentence. 'T. S. Eliot' by contrast, being male, will be so fully titled only at the outset. From then on he is, more economically, 'Eliot'. Such is the old convention but it is increasingly being challenged.

Does this formula imply that men can speak on behalf of all humanity but women are confined to writing as women? Or does the use of a woman's full name positively suggest a more humanly accessible, less loftily remote, voice? Or might the convention be no more than a quaintly old-fashioned, and harmless, gesture of courtesy? Could it, on the other hand, be firmly placing women on a pedestal where their room for independent manoeuvre will be severely limited? Does the succinctness with which male authors can be mentioned imply the untruth that their works have proved more lastingly significant than texts by their female contemporaries, and so the well-informed reader will need less guidance to identify them? In fact Jane Austen is now far more widely read than Sir Walter Scott but your tutor may still reject 'Austen' as inadequate while accepting 'Scott' as a sensible economy. Think about it. Then, whether you conform to the old discrimination or embrace the new equity, you will know what you are doing and be ready to defend it.

Many of the most frequently taught works of literature do construct men and women as essentially different in their aspirations and their abilities. A few texts may enforce sexual stereotyping by bullyingly obvious methods but the majority are more discreetly manipulative. Your essay might, for instance, need to observe where and how some text suggests that its own voice should be heard as masculine or feminine rather than neutrally human. The work under discussion may also subtly portray its ideal reader as a man or a woman. Often your essay should be identifying those literary devices that implicitly support some squalid or idiotic myth about half of our species. Do check that your own prose has not imitatively stumbled into using any of the sexist techniques that it discusses.

6 Presentation

Rough draft into fair copy

If time allows, you should write out your essay in a two-stage process. First, compose a provisional, but complete, draft of all that you intend to say. Think of this not as a 'rough copy' but as a 'working draft'. Do work at it, making additions, deletions and corrections as you write. Add relevant ideas. Cut obscurities and padding. Substitute clearer terms in which to convey your meaning.

A first draft allows you to make as many alterations as spring to mind without your being inhibited by the growing messiness. However inelegant this version may start to look as you cross out some words and squeeze in others, it will still be decipherable by you; and only you need to see it.

When you have written out the last sentence of this working draft, read it all through from the beginning. Thoughtfully review and thoroughly revise. Try to find a friend or relative who is prepared to listen while you read it aloud, to ask questions where puzzled, and to offer constructive advice. At least try reading it aloud to yourself. Then you will be able to hear where it sounds confusing in structure or clumsy in style. When you can find no more opportunities for improvement or when there is simply no more time, write out the essay again as a fair copy.

Think of the adjective 'fair' here as a pun. Good-looking work may find favour. An essay which looks beautiful will not, of course, be forgiven for talking nonsense. Yet an ugly one may be thought to contain less sense than it in fact does.

Troubling to produce a fair copy also shows your sense of fair play. You are asking someone to help you. You want your criticism to be carefully studied. You want detailed advice on how it can be improved. So there is simple justice in being courteously considerate and providing an easily accessible route into your work.

In circumstances where there cannot be time for both a full rough draft and a fair copy – examinations, for instance, – at least ensure that every word of the essay is legible.

Preliminaries on the first page

Write out your reader's name at the top of the page: perhaps on the left-hand side. Write out your name: top right is a widely accepted format. Also identify some grouping to which you belong: the title of the particular course which you are follow-ing or the number of the year which you have reached in it. Finally, write out in full the set title or question exactly as it was given to you. Then leave a space of at least one line between this and your first sentence. Number this sheet '1' and all others in sequence.

Leave space for comments

Conventions of precisely how much space you should offer, and where, do vary. Find out what practice your tutor prefers. In all cases, there must be ample room for your reader to offer two different kinds of advice.

You should welcome specific comments about the more localized means and effects of your essay. So provide an extra margin throughout. If the paper which you are using has a printed margin, you could double it so that there is twice as much space on the left-hand side. Alternatively you could offer an extra margin on the right by stopping early on each line. Also, leave a space equivalent to two, or even three, lines at the foot of every page. This can then be used for lengthier comments on the material above.

At the end of the entire essay leave room for response to the work as a whole. Be optimistic. Allow one-third or even half of a page so that the tutor can easily offer as much constructive advice as time allows.

Titles of literary works

The title of any published book should be underlined. This is the hand-written equivalent of the printer's italics. So what you must write out as <u>The Mill on the Floss</u>, a printed essay would present as *The Mill on the Floss*. The rule applies not only to novels but also to any play, any work of discursive prose, any long poem or collection of shorter ones which, on its first publication, constituted a single, printed book.

Where a shorter work first appeared along with others as only one component of a volume, its title should not be underlined. Instead, it should be placed in single quotation marks. So the title of Blake's song about London is distinguished from the name of the city itself by being written as 'London'. In this case, the title which you should underline is <u>Songs of Experience</u>, the collection of poems among which 'London' was first printed.

Failure to underline the title of a major work can seriously mislead. Where you write of Hamlet or Robinson Crusoe or Don Juan, your reader must assume you to mean that fictional character. Only when underlined as <u>Hamlet</u>, <u>Robinson Crusoe</u> and <u>Don Juan</u> will they be seen as referring to entire texts.

Place names too can confuse. If you mention Middlemarch, your reader will think that you mean the town in which George Eliot sets her novel. The novel itself is written as <u>Middlemarch</u>. So, too, Wuthering Heights and Bleak House are the names of houses. The texts which describe those houses are called <u>Wuthering Heights</u> and <u>Bleak House</u>.

To avoid confusion with underlined titles, you must not underline any of your own words or phrases for emphasis. Instead, indicate which should carry most weight by redesigning the syntax of your sentence.

For similar reasons, only the title of a short work or an actual quotation should be enclosed in quotation marks. These must not be used to apologize for any of your own terminology. If you are in doubt as to whether a word that you want to include is correct English or strictly accurate, pause. First try to find some expression which is undoubtedly appropriate and use that instead. If you cannot think of one and must settle for the dubious term, do not add quotation marks. Their defensiveness will merely draw attention to the vulnerable phrasing and virtually guarantee its being attacked.

Titles of scholarly and critical works

Titles of book-length works should again be underlined. So should the titles of periodicals. Titles of shorter essays and reviews which together compose a book or a periodical should not be underlined. They should be preceded and followed by a single quotation mark. So Marilyn Butler's book (on English literature and its background in the period 1760–1830) should be described as <u>Romantics, Rebels and Reactionaries</u>. Her two-page review article (about books on Wordsworth) should, on the other hand, have its title placed in quotation marks: 'Three feet on the ground', <u>London Review of Books</u>, 14–20 April 1983. Note that the title of the journal in which the essay was published is underlined.

Quotations

Make sure that all your quotations are copied out with strict accuracy.

Sometimes, to increase economy and help your reader to concentrate upon what is most relevant to your present point, you may want to omit some portion of the original passage. If so, hesitate. Ensure that no significant misrepresentations will be involved. Where you decide to go ahead and make the omission, indicate it clearly with an ellipsis: three full stops preceded and followed by a space (. . .).

Try to be meticulous about punctuation, capital letters and spelling. The correct spelling is, of course, that adopted by the text, regardless of modern practice.

Accuracy is more important than any of the other rules about quotations which are given below. Where you break any of the following conventions about where and how to set out extracts on the page, you may seem ignorant of, or careless about, the formalities of literary criticism. But if you misquote, you will sound casual about literature itself. At worst, your reader may begin to wonder whether you are interested in discovering and expressing the truth.

There are two different formats by which to indicate that you are ceasing to write your own prose and are now reproducing an extract from a text. One is for a brief quotation: no more than twenty words of prose or two complete lines of verse. The other is for more substantial extracts.

Shorter quotations should be distinguished from your own prose simply by being enclosed in single quotation marks. In extracts from poems, line endings must be identified by an oblique stroke:

> Byron's journals suggest impatience with modern poetry. Keats's verse, for instance, is disdained as 'a sort of mental masturbation' (*Letters and Journals*, Vol. VII, p. 225). Wordsworth, however, is a less dismissible enigma: a 'stupendous genius' if also a 'damned fool' (Vol. V, p. 13). In *Childe Harolde*, Byron himself tries out a Wordsworthian pantheism: 'Are not the mountains, waves and skies, a part/Of me . . . ?' (Canto III, stanza 75). The question, however, may not be merely rhetorical. The Alpine landscape, only a few stanzas earlier, has been said 'to show/How earth may pierce to Heaven, yet leave vain man below' (III, 62).

A longer quotation is set clearly apart from your own sentences. The correct layout is that which I have just used above in quoting from an essay on Byron. The sentence which introduces the quotation should end in a colon. Then your pen should move down to a new line and write the first word of the quotation at least one inch further to the right than the margin you are using for your own prose. Every ensuing line of the quotation should be indented to this same extent. Each line should also end earlier than lines of your own prose. The quotation is thus framed by additional margins on both sides. Note that the first line of the above extract is no more indented than those that follow. This signals that the quotation does not begin at the point where the original text starts a new

paragraph. Had I written the quotation's first word a little
more to the right than the first word of the following lines, I
would have been claiming that the extract begins where the
original text begins a fresh paragraph.

Where your substantial extract is from a work in verse, the
lines will normally be short enough to create the extra space
required on the right-hand side. Where they are not, maintain
the space by writing out the last few words of each line just
below:

> As the husband is, the wife is: thou art mated with a
>   clown,
> And the grossness of his nature will have weight to drag
>   thee down.
>
> He will hold thee, when his passion shall have spent its
>   novel force,
> Something better than his dog, a little dearer than his
>   horse.
>
> (Tennyson, 'Locksley Hall', ll. 47–50)

You must reproduce the text's own typography as far as
possible. In the example above, for instance, the poem inserts
an extra space between each pair of rhyming lines. This may
advise the reader on how to shape the poem, interpreting it as
a series of couplets rather than some more seamless fabric. So,
in quoting the four lines, I have reproduced the extra space
between the second and third.

Reproduce the varying degrees of indentation which the text
chooses to allocate to different lines:

> "How strange is human pride!
> I tell thee that those living things,
> To whom the fragile blade of grass,
>   That springeth in the morn
>   And perisheth ere noon,
>   Is an unbounded world;
> I tell thee that those viewless beings,
> Whose mansion is the smallest particle
> Of the impassive atmosphere,
>   Think, feel and live like man;
> That their affections and antipathies,

> Like his, produce the laws
> Ruling their moral state;
> And the minutest throb
> That through their frame diffuses
> The slightest, faintest motion,
> Is fixed and indispensable
> As the majestic laws
> That rule yon rolling orbs."
>
> (Shelley, *Queen Mab*, ll. 225–43)

The double quotation marks here are reproduced from the text itself where they are used to denote that the lines are direct speech by one of the poem's characters. Never add any quotation marks of your own to extracts which are long enough to be set apart from your prose.

Identify the source of each quotation

Give a clear reference for even the briefest one-word quotation. Then, if the reader should doubt its accuracy or feel curious about its context, there will be precise guidance on where to find the relevant passage in the original text.

The reference for short quotations which are embedded in one of your own sentences can be placed either immediately after the quotation or at the end of the sentence. Enclose it in brackets.

The reference for long, indented quotations must be given at the end of each extract. It should be bracketed and placed on a line of its own to the right-hand end.

In neither case are there any universally accepted, rigid rules about how full these references should be. However, the guidelines are these. Be accurate. Be clear. Be brief. Where you have not referred to a text before in the essay and it is not a well-known work, you may need to describe it almost as fully as is required for your formal bibliography. Far more often, you can provide sufficient guidance by just giving the number of a chapter, page or line.

If you look back to the above extract from an essay on Byron, you will see that the first quotation from *Childe Harolde* spells out what the numerals represent: 'Canto III, stanza 75'. This may be necessary as otherwise the reader might momentarily think that you mean line numbers. The second reference, however, can afford to gain the brevity of 'III, 62', relying on the reader to have understood that the roman numerals refer to cantos and the arabic ones to stanzas.

Notice, too, that neither reference gives the title of the poem. This should always be included where there could be any doubt. Here there is none because the first quotation is offered in a sentence beginning 'In *Childe Harolde*'. By contrast in offering the quotation from Shelley's *Queen Mab*, I could not reasonably expect you to deduce from my context what work, or even what author, I would be quoting. My reference therefore supplies both, as well as identifying the passage's position in the text by line numbers.

For extracts from plays, it is safest to give the numbers of act, scene and lines. The act is identified first in large roman numerals (I, II, III, IV, V); then the scene in small roman numerals (i, ii, iii, iv, v, vi, vii, etc.); finally the line numbers in arabic numerals: 'Lear himself has described the division of the kingdom as a "darker purpose" (I. ii. 36)'. Where your context leaves no possibility of doubt about which scene you mean, you can just identify the relevant line: 'In the very first scene of the play, Lear calls the division a "darker purpose" (36)'. If either of these sentences appears in an essay whose topic is clearly *King Lear*, the play's title need not be repeated within the reference.

You might, however, momentarily need to quote *King Lear* in an essay on some quite different work. Then the title, too, would need to be included in the reference:

> Hardy's characters sometimes seem like the victims of some cosmic, practical joker. *Tess of the D'Urbervilles* remorselessly teases and tortures its heroine until the very last page. It is only in the closing paragraph that 'The President of the Immortals' is said to have finished his 'sport' with Tess. She has at last escaped further torment by being killed. Hardy's zestfully bitter image recalls some of Shakespeare's bleakest lines: 'As flies to wanton boys, are we to th' Gods;/They kill us for their sport' (*King Lear*, IV. i. 36–7).

Note that the quotation from Hardy's own text is here given no reference. The context guides the reader unmistakably to *Tess of the D'Urbervilles* and to that novel's 'last paragraph'.

All the conventions for presenting quotations do, of course, apply just as much to extracts from critical or scholarly works as to those from primary sources. So, where you are quoting a critical book and your introductory sentence does name the critic ('X suggests that'; 'Y argues:'), your bracketed reference after the quotation only needs to give title and page number. For fuller information your reader will look to your bibliography.

Bibliography

After the last sentence of your essay and before the space which you must leave for your tutor's comments, add a bibliography. This is a list of all the texts which you have found useful in composing your essay.

There are only two ways in which you must get the bibliography right. Firstly, make it complete. Include the edition which you have been using to study each of the literary works which your essay mentions. Without this information your reader cannot use the references in the main body of your essay to find each quotation in the original text. Page numbers of works in prose – and often line numbers of those in verse – vary from edition to edition.

Do not forget any work of criticism or scholarship which you have consulted and found relevant. Even the briefest article which supplied only one useful observation must be listed. However, you must not rely upon your bibliography to prove that you are innocent of plagiarism. Merely listing a book or essay at the end cannot define precisely where, and how far, your own argument is indebted to it. Spell that out clearly within the main body of your essay at the precise point where the borrowed material is being used.

The second necessity is that your bibliography should be clear. The reader must be able to see precisely which books you mean, and to understand in exactly what issue of what periodical a given article can be found. Imagine your tutor going to the library in search of some text which you have listed. In the case of a book, have you made the author's full name and the work's title so clear that it can be instantly identified in the library catalogue? In the case of a review in some weekly journal like *The Times Literary Supplement*, can the right issue be sought immediately or must a whole shelf of back-numbers be searched? Have you been considerate enough to specify on which page of the relevant week's issue the article begins?

Provided that your bibliography is both comprehensive and comprehensible, your tutor will not mind too much about its detailed format. However, as the agreed conventions are easy enough, you may as well take a professional pride in learning them. For books, the entry should list the following items in this order:

1) The author's surname.
2) The author's forename or initials.
   Neither name should be underlined. The exception is where the book is the text of an established writer's literary works. If the title of the book includes that writer's name, ignore items 1 and 2 above, beginning the entry in your bibliography with the title: *The Complete Poetical Works of Shelley* or *Coleridge's Verse: A Selection*. You then proceed with item 4 below and so on.
3) The work's full title. Here, as elsewhere, this must be underlined.
4) Where applicable, the name of the editor(s) or translator(s) preceded by 'ed.' or 'trans.'.
5) Where applicable, the number of volumes into which the work is divided for ease of printing and handling. Thus items 3, 4 and 5 could be: *The Poetical Works of William Wordsworth*, ed. E. de Selincourt and Helen Darbishire (5 vols).
6) The place and date of publication. Optionally, the name of the publisher can be included: either before, or in between, these two.

Conventions as to what punctuation should appear between these items vary. Your tutor will not object to full stops, commas, semi-colons or even brackets provided that their positioning does not reduce clarity. Equally adequate versions are:

Hammond, Gerald, *The Reader and Shakespeare's Young Man Sonnets*, London, 1981.

Hammond, Gerald. *The Reader and Shakespeare's Young Man Sonnets*. Macmillan (London, 1981).

However, the Modern Language Association's format for punctuation is becoming increasingly accepted. This is: *Title* (place: publisher, date): e.g. *The Reader and Shakespeare's Young Man Sonnets* (London: Macmillan, 1981).

For articles in all periodicals (ranging from daily newspapers to quarterly, or even annual, publications by learned societies), the sequence should be:

1) The surname of the article's author.
2) Forename or initials of article's author.
3) Title of article, not underlined, but enclosed in single quotation marks.
4) Title of periodical underlined.
5) Where applicable, volume number. This is usually given on the front cover in large roman numerals following either the word Volume or its abbreviation (Vol.).
6) Date at which relevant issue appeared. Follow the periodical's own degree of specificity. *The Times Literary Supplement*, for instance, is a weekly and identifies each issue by printing the day of the month, the month and the year of its publication. *Critical Quarterly* on the other hand uses the four seasons, describing an issue as 'Summer 1980' or 'Spring 1983'. Monthly magazines tend to give just month and year.
7) Page numbers for that portion of the issue which is occupied by the cited article.

Examples are:

Rudrum, Alan: 'Polygamy in *Paradise Lost*'; *Essays in Criticism*, Vol. XX, January 1970, pp. 18–23.
White, R. S., 'Shakespearean music in Keats' "Ode to a Nightingale"', *English*, Volume XXX (Autumn 1981): pp. 217–25.

Note that again punctuation, provided that it is not misleading, is variable. Observe too the way the titles of literary works are correctly presented in both cases: Keats's 'Ode to a Nightingale' was first published with other poems in a volume of 1820: it is placed in quotation marks. *Paradise Lost* first appeared as a book on its own, so it is underlined.

Tutor's comments

With your bibliography completed, your essay should finally be presentable and can be submitted to your tutor. Yet that moment is only the end of one phase and the beginning of another.

Most obviously, but perhaps least importantly, this essay may eventually be awarded a mark. Remember that different teachers, even when they are working in the same institution, can mean quite different things by any alphabetical or numerical label attached to an essay. Some will mark roughly according to the standards of a Finals examiner, and some far more generously. Others may use a flexible system of carrot-and-stick, adapting their mark-scale so as to motivate a particular student at a given stage of the course. A few will be downright casual about what mark they allocate and instead concentrate all their efforts on supplying detailed and constructive responses to your ideas and their expression.

You should pay most attention to comments. These may anyway be a far better guide to how well you have done than the mark can be. Once you have your tutor's reactions, your thoughts should already be turning to how much better you can do next time. Use your teacher's remarks to think further about the topic and to appreciate issues which you had underestimated or even ignored when you were writing the essay. Look, too, for any guidance on how your structure or style might be improved and resolve to reconsider that advice while you are actually working on your next piece of criticism.

If you are uncertain as to whether you have fully understood some comment, do seek clarification. The enterprise of all literary critics is sometimes described as a communal debate and certainly the progress of the apprentice-critic should depend on a dialogue with the teacher. You must overcome any laziness or shyness which might prevent you from ever initiating that dialogue. Often you will have doubts, curiosities, wishes or even simple needs of reassurance that your tutor may not be able to guess.

To reveal these may, on occasion, seem daunting. Beforehand, it may take an uncomfortable amount of intellectual effort to discover precisely how your problem should be defined. It may then require an unfamiliar degree of boldness to speak up and spell it out. Force yourself to develop such qualities. It is not just students aiming to make good use of their teachers who need to acquire such strengths. Energy of thought and courage of expression should be among the essential aims of all who face the problems, and enjoy the privilege, of writing literary criticism.

7 Postscript on pleasure

Looking back on this little book, I note how much of it has been devoted to the difficulties and mere practicalities of writing critical essays, and how little space has been found in which to evoke its pleasures. This may have been inevitable. Perhaps a similar unease is felt by those who have written short guides to other activities such as playing football, or appreciating opera, or being a social worker or making love. In these, as in literary criticism, many skills and satisfactions in fact derive more from instinct and a sensitively flexible response to each occasion's localized demands than from intellectual rules which have been consciously learnt. So let me close by privileging pleasure through a rule against rules. If you repeatedly find that following any guideline – even one of those that I myself have suggested in the preceding pages – is actually diminishing your pleasure in writing critical essays, abandon it. Of course literary criticism can – and perhaps should – aspire to serve one or other of those high-minded causes that are often cited as its justification. But such a cause will best be served in works written with the vigour of enthusiasm by those who have learnt that composing a critical essay can be fun.